POWERSHELL

"The Ultimate Guide To Learning And Understanding Powershell Programming"

By

Robert Clarke

Table of Contents

INTRODUCTION 5

WHAT IS POWERSHELL 11

   User's Guide To Powershell 24

POWERSHELL HISTORY 37

FEATURES OF POWERSHELL... 43

HOW TO LAUNCH POWERSHELL 70

POWERSHELL CMDLET...76

CMDLET VS COMMAND..93

HOW TO RESOLVE "OVERLAP: DUPLICATE OWNERSHIP FOR
DIRECTORY" ERROR IN WINDOWS 100

POWERSHELL DATA TYPES 105

POWERSHELL SCRIPTS 134

MODULES 174

PACKAGES 183

POWERSHELL CONCEPTS 226

POWERSHELL VS COMMAND PROMPT.............................. 248

APPLICATIONS OF POWERSHELL....................................... 259

   Ways To View And Save List Of Updates Installed On
Windows 10... 266

CONCLUSION 275

INTRODUCTION

Imagine you are working on a project to upgrade your home, but you don't have all the resources you need. You ask a friend to bring a Hex screwdriver, a friend, and your cousin for a hammer. Your project is ineffective and complicated to date. Now, imagine that you are working on the same project, but now you have a toolbox, an infinitely large toolbox filled with all the tools available. That's what PowerShell works like.

As of 2008, PowerShell has been a Windows system horse for scripting/system management, which most users do not learn, since it uses Visual User Interfaces (GUI) instead of Command-Line Interfaces (CLI). PowerShell can do everything the GUI does, and it can be done remotely, instantly, and repeatable. PowerShell is a CLI incorporating DOS command, Windows Script Hosting (WSH), JScript, VB script, and COM (Component Object Model),.NET, and C #direct code manipulation. All of these can be run seamlessly together, bypassing object-oriented programming models and in a pipeline system like Unix, where several commands can be fastened together to ensure that the output is the input of one command. These pipelines can create a single line of code for numerous complex repetitive tasks.

PowerShell's main power lies in the sheer volume and caliber of PowerShell's add-ons, Cmdlets (command-lets). These are like old tools or executables, except now they can be downloaded on request. Microsoft dedicated its APIs to be made accessible through PowerShell. PowerShell's current version is Version 4, which Microsoft has continually added to and extended its reach, capacity, functionality, and resilience. You may start the remote command on machines that are properly configured to communicate with Active Directories or other data sources (SQL, DB, XML, text, registry, WMI, etc.). It is based on Windows 8 by default but can be enabled on Windows OS from XP.

Try some basic file operations such as "DIR," "CD," "Cd\" and "C:" when using PowerShell first time, and you will find that all standard DOS operations are similar. However, when you first try to run the. EXE file, you will find that it does not work. PowerShell only makes the application with a path notion, so add a ".\" in front of the program file name, and PowerShell would know what to do with the script.

PowerShell is an integrated Windows utility with a wide scripting language. When you write.bat files for command-line operation, everything PowerShell can do will impress you. Please note I'm not (yet) a master of PowerShell. But I'm so fascinated by the fact that I'm working with it that I decided to bring it to faithful WindowsTip readers. You can start PowerShell somehow in a variety of ways, and it depends on which version of Windows you are running. Although I'm going to mention different ways of activating this, I will concentrate on using PowerShell on the command line. One way to invoke PowerShell is to open the Command Line window (which is protected by a specific tip) and enter the "PowerShell" form (without the quote marks). Another way to search for "Windows PowerShell" on a search engine is to use the search capabilities of Windows and pick the "Windows PowerShell ISE" search result. When you choose this object, a split-screen will appear, where you can interactively enter PowerShell commands in the bottom of the screen, and also generate a PowerShell script file in the top of the screen.

PowerShell is a command-line shell specially designed for system administrators from Windows. Windows

PowerShell provides an interactive prompt and an independent scripting environment. Windows PowerShell introduces the Cmdlet framework, a simple, single-function, shell-built command-line tool. Windows PowerShell is a Windows computer command-line interface. A CLI is a program to tell the machine to perform tasks with typed commands. This allows the automation of tasks and doing several things with one instruction. Windows PowerShell is a command-line evolution–integrating a DOS shell with the scripting environment. It can help with repetitive tasks, processes that work simultaneously on many files, automate and program tasks, and configure Windows components and services. PowerShell is not only much more versatile than running DOS commands. It facilitates complex decision taking, links to several data sources, and the development of even graphical user interfaces. It is now a core competency for IT and server administrators. It is now a basic prerequisite/ability for a system administrator.

The latest version is version 2.0 and was released publicly on 28 October 2009. We say shell and script language because you can use these components separately. It is a command-based shell on the fundamental level of the console-like interface, which allows you to issue commands and call out its powerful scripting language for what tasks you need to accomplish. In this collaborative application, you issue commands directly to the console and execute the necessary tasks. The additional powerful part of PowerShell that benefits from the underlying scripting language are the ability to perform longer or more complex script instructions. It helps you to execute some of the functions automatically. The last brand new aspect of version 2.0 is the ability to execute commands on one or more machines on a single PowerShell computer. Together, these skills will allow you to work almost without problems.

Another thing to be familiar with is PowerShell's command syntax. The PowerShell commands are called cmdlets. These simple instructions allow you to carry out all the common system management tasks. All cmdlets share a similar syntax of a verb and a noun in a verb-noun format. For instance, we use one of the most helpful commands, get-help. Cmdlet is a simple example. Type help, followed by the topic or command you wish to get help with, will provide you with more information. It gives you the support you need or gives you a list of topics to narrow it down to the one you need.

You will have a chance to try a few cmdlets of your own later in this guide, but you have to look at it if you don't have it before.

As you can see, the main objective of Windows PowerShell is to provide the system administrator with greater control and facilitate the performance of the required tasks. It improves the tool bag of the administrator by incorporating automation and removal and their associated benefits. Only imagine having to write a command once and then run it on different machines several times. It removes the need to run the same thing over and over just by having PowerShell run it several times. It also removes certain aspects of human error because you only have to write it once and only review it once. We will cover many of the new Windows Server 2008 R2 commands in this tutorial and try to give you a feel for it and what they are meant to do.

WHAT IS POWERSHELL

PowerShell is a Microsoft automation application and scripting language. It includes a shell and scripting language command-line that is embedded within the. Net framework and can be incorporated into other applications. It is a task-based command-line shell that automates batch processing and helps build tools for system management. It is a combination of versatile scripting, speed of the control line, and GUI-based admin strength. Any issue can be effectively overcome by helping systems to get rid of potential manual working hours.

This is known for the convergence of ideas in many ways. All these definitions are like programming shells. To grasp the conventional command-line interfaces, it is necessary to know that they are configured for handling different objects. An object is a piece of structured information that can be accessed directly by this object syntax in portions of data. It has a large family of commands that can be expanded. It has interfaces like cmd.exe that help to extend the built-in commands indirectly. The native commands are called cmdlets. The user will build their cmdlet modules and functions using cmdlets. These modules can easily add

11

cmdlets and shell providers. PowerShell also supports scripts that are similar to Unix scripts.

PowerShell's success is because it gives Windows Command Prompt more power, versatility, and flexibility. Since it is not possible to do everything through GUI, the command line is very necessary. You can quickly change the active directory attributes for thousands of users using PowerShell. The user of PowerShell can easily complete the task with a single code line. It is a system that provides the server with an interactive framework. The PowerShell command is interactive, allowing you to execute different commands in real-time. It's easier and faster because no script has to be modified on the notepad and then executed separately. However, the user will invoke all small scripts, bat files, or procedures. These can all be cited by PowerShell. It is said to be a strong instrument. This ability to recall all the commands is not feasible or realistic. This is right in the editor, where several resources will help you get the right solution.

By using this, a user can easily run and build scripts. The user must open and edit Windows PowerShell in the script pane that provides specific types of files. Such files are classified as files for the script(.ps1), data files for the script(.psd1), and module files for the script (.psm1). These types of files are assigned in the script pane to different colors. Configuration files, XML files, and text files may be included in other files. A developer can easily build a new script file, open existing scripts, close any window, and so on. You can easily view the file path, run the script, or even execute part of the script. This user also allows the text to be entered in the script window, copied and updated. It does not require programming knowledge. By using the Exchange server consumer, such tasks from the command line can be triggered. It is also useful for managers who want to learn to write. When cmdlets are learned, they may work with individual components and products. The scripts are interchangeable, and these run combinations depend on certain requirements. Such scripts can be used to build different frameworks.

PowerShell is a Microsoft-based process automation and set-up management system consisting of a command-line shell and associated scripting language. At first, it was just a Windows component called Windows PowerShell, which was made open-source and cross-pattern by the launch of PowerShell Core on 18 August 2016.

In PowerShell, administrative tasks are usually performed by specialized cmdlets. NET classes are performing a particular operation. This works by accessing data in different data stores such as the file system or registry made available by providers to PowerShell. Third-party developers can add PowerShell cmdlets and providers. Scripts can use cmdlets, and scripts can be packaged into modules.

PowerShell provides full access to both the COM and the WMI so that administrative tasks can be performed on both local and remote Windows systems, WS-Management, and the CIM so that remote Linux and network devices can be handled. PowerShell also offers a hosting API that enables PowerShell to run in other devices. These applications can then use the PowerShell features, including operations exposed can graphic interface, to implement those operations. Microsoft Exchange Server 2007 used this capability to reveal its management features as PowerShell cmdlets and providers and to introduce the graphic administration tools as PowerShell hosting systems that invoke the necessary cmdlets. Their management framework via PowerShell cmdlets is also shown by other

Microsoft applications, including Microsoft SQL server 2008.

PowerShell has its robust console-based support, which can be accessed from the Get-Help cmdlet (similar to man pages in Unix shells). Local support content can be accessed via the Update-Help cmdlet from the internet. Instead, web assistance can be accessed case-by-case via. The script component of the web is similar to Perl programming. The shell is similar to UNIX, with commands like man, ls, and ps included by Microsoft for convenience. PowerShell 1.0 was introduced in Windows XP SP2, Windows Server 2003 SP1, Windows Vista in November 2006. Although PowerShell must first be enabled manually, Windows 10 is the default version 5.0. You can, therefore, go to Cortana and type' PowerShell' or search the Start menu. Read more about which version of Windows that PowerShell uses.

PowerShell is also supplied with a built-in scripting environment (ISE). The ISE screen is divided into two parts–the top one is used to write the script and the bottom for commands manually. The ISE provides a GUI interface with insightful syntax recommendations, painting, tab completion, and error handling.

PowerShell is your tool if you are a Windows administrator that often needs to perform user management, DNS set-up, and other tedious tasks.WHY USE POWERSHELL

Sometimes when it comes to designing websites, you need things to work for you automatically. It's not that it's hard to deploy them, it's routine. It may be simpler for you to write a short script that will do the work for you at some stage. PowerShell will come in there. PowerShell is a game-changer when you have access to the server on that platform. If you have tasks you want to run automatically to control operating systems and their processes, you can consider using PowerShell. So each time you press a particular button, you might write a script that changes someone's history. Or you can write a script that restarts the process of your website after all the files are uploaded. PowerShell is now extremely popular with many IT managers because of its ability to automate management processes and streamline efforts. Managers of large networks can deploy solutions such as security patches or other software upgrades over a huge network of computers or servers to ensure the proper installation and operation of the service or solution, without logging into every single machine. One PowerShell script is all it takes to act.

The development of a PowerShell script is quite easy. Only open a file and write your code and save it. These scripts are provided by a.ps1 extension. You can run your script manually or program it to perform regular administration tasks automatically. IT administrators have an easy and efficient way to install applications, track and collect data about servers, and control processes, files, and records using PowerShell commands and scripts. And although it is impossible to list the many features of PowerShell, they are readily available and easy to find. Once you have gone through the initial learning curve, you can use these powerful features and become a superuser!

The barrier to learning PowerShell because of its near-ubiquity is relatively low. You should type "PowerShell" into your search box if your PC runs Windows 10 to get instant access to PowerShell's Windows PowerShell program. Although most people use a GUI to communicate with their computers, they also provide a text-based interface called a "command-line interface" (CLI) to create commands.

PowerShell is the built-in IT administrators ' CLI for Microsoft Windows that allow desk staff to:

Automate redundant tasks

Handle IT environments at scale

Access user information that is difficult to find

There are many applications for PowerShell if you have a lot of processes that need to run under certain conditions at certain times, and you do not want to wait until each process starts the next one. If you need to report on the same data every time, you can even do stuff such as converting Excel files to Word.

Another important reason you could use PowerShell is if you want to keep the processes stable. Once a script is written, every time it is executed, the same thing. You don't need to worry about missing a move or somewhere getting a man. It even produces logs so that you can monitor errors at each step of the process.

For many MSPs, PowerShell is a popular tool, as it helps to simplify management tasks and generate insights into devices, especially in medium and large networks. Here is how PowerShell uses the workflow to transform:

It's not going away any time soon

Microsoft has shown that PowerShell is staying here. PowerShell version 2 is currently not only included in

Windows Server 2008 R2 and allowed by default in Windows 7. Part of Microsoft's explanation is that many additional products will be built on PowerShell in the future.

Most Microsoft products will eventually use it

Virtually all server products Microsoft produces can be handled through PowerShell right now. From an administrative point of view, this means that you have the skills required to manage most of the newer Microsoft products if you are competent in PowerShell. The basic PowerShell commands are used for all PowerShell items. Nevertheless, some application products have additional cmdlets in PowerShell.

You can't do everything from the GUI any more

When Microsoft developed exchange 2007, it built the Interface for the most popular administrative functions. Some unknown or potentially destructive tasks must be carried out with PowerShell. This design philosophy is supposed to be applied to other Microsoft products.

It can make your life easier

Believe it or not, it can make your life more comfortable with the command line. Suppose for a moment you need to change a thousand user Active Directory attribute. The job will probably take hours to complete manually. However, you can complete the task with PowerShell using a single line of code.

Many GUIs are PowerShell front ends

Many of the GUI interfaces developed by Microsoft for its different products are simply PowerShell's front end interfaces. The Exchange Management Console is probably the best-known example of this. While this tool looks like a standard management tool, it is entirely built on PowerShell. Every operation performed by the GUI produces PowerShell code to complete the requested task. The console also shows you in many cases the PowerShell command used to complete the task.

Microsoft certification exams contain PowerShell questions

Too many of its recent certification exams, Microsoft has applied PowerShell-specific questions. My experience with these tests was that, but you need to know which command you should use in a given situation, you do not have to learn the full command syntax.

You can use PowerShell commands to manage your domains

You should install the Active Directory Web Services on at least one Domain Controller if you have domain controllers running Windows Server 2003 with or beyond Service Pack 2. After that, you can use the Windows 7 RSAT Suite to handle Windows 2003 and Windows 2008.

It enables interactivity between products

PowerShell is the common thread among all of the latest Microsoft server products, so I expect to start seeing PowerShell used as an interaction mechanism between server products. A real-world example of this interactivity is still to be seen, but I would expect to be able to work seamlessly with products like IIS, SQL Server, and Share with a PowerShell script.

Microsoft says it's important

Just because someone says that something is essential in Microsoft, that doesn't mean I take it as gospel. But in

TechNet Magazine's October 2009 version, Microsoft says, "It is safe to say that the only important skill a Windows administrator requires in the coming years is expertise in Windows PowerShell." This is especially true because this statement represents what I've learned from different people in Microsoft every time I visited Redmond lately.

If you don't learn it, someone else will

The economy is in a recession, as we all know, and many businesses are shrinking. Of course, there is a lot of competition for the few open IT workers. If you are unexpectedly looking for another job, then your chance of finding one could be higher if you can use PowerShell.

Easy Automation

Windows PowerShell introduces a cmdlet, a simple, single-function command-line tool incorporated into the shell (pronounced command-let). You can use each cmdlet individually, but its strength is enhanced if you combine these simple tools with complex tasks.

Windows PowerShell includes over a hundred basic cmdlets, and you can write and share your cmdlets with other users. Cmdlets and PowerShell scripting are in-demand skills for small and large businesses throughout North America and Europe. Recent searches on the "PowerShell Jobs" page on Dice.com have resulted in nearly 2000 open positions in just 15 locations across the United States.

Scalable Management

We know that it takes a few clicks to install operating system updates on a PC. Nonetheless, it can take time to install these upgrades on only a decade of laptops and a great desktop PC in a small office. Imagine how long you need to upgrade 563 PCs in a few places— without impacting the workforce's overall productivity.

Smart IT administrators use PowerShell to write a cmdlet to execute a task more than a few times. All you can do in PowerShell with a few mouse clicks on the GUI can be done faster.

Accessing Information

Like many CLIs, PowerShell provides access to the computer's filesystem. PowerShell providers also allow you to access data and information that are hard to access. IT managers, for example, can use PowerShell to access secure data stores like the Windows registry and digital signature certificates quickly.

This is critical because PowerShell is designed above Microsoft. NET Framework, as opposed to most CLIs. It is a unique feature that allows This professional to automate and execute special tasks remotely on any Windows PC in the company's network. Best of all, by typing a command-line file, PowerShell gives IT administrators deep visibility and control of all those network resources.

PowerShell is also a significant part of managing Microsoft Office 365 enterprise deployments. Many important PowerShell management commands are not available on the Office 365 web portal. For example, in Office 365, the default Business choice is either for every user to change passwords regularly or for no one ever to change their passwords. Amaxra uses PowerShell to allow individual Office 365 users in our organization to skip password changes frequently by using two-factor authentication. We wouldn't be able to change Office 365's default password choices without PowerShell.

You've undoubtedly heard of PowerShell if you wrestled with Windows 10. If you've been trying to do something sophisticated lately with Win7/8.1, it's possibly also PowerShell. After years on the Windows command line and accumulated batch files, it is time to look at something more efficient, more flexible— better.

PowerShell is a huge addition to the Windows toolbox and can cause some fear because of the enormity of it. Is it the language of the book, a command base, a floor wax? Do you need to bind a cmdlet to an instantiated.net class to run with providers? And why all support talk about administrators — must I be a qualified Windows administrator to use them?

The guide below is for those who want to use PowerShell. Find it to be a radical transition from PowerShell to PowerShell, which is interesting.

Crank it up

PowerShell itself is the first thing you will need. If you use Windows 10, PowerShell 5, the latest version, has already been installed. (There is a 5.1 Win10 Anniversary Update, but you don't know the difference with the 5.0 Fall Update)

PowerShell 4 Windows 8 and 8.1, which is kind enough to get your feet wet. PowerShell is not difficult to install on Windows 7, but it takes extra care–it has to be installed separately. Juan Pablo Jofre discusses how to install WMF 5.0, which contains PowerShell, in addition to the devices that are unlikely to be used when you start it on MSDN.

PowerShell provides two interfaces. The full-blown Interface, known as the integrated scripting environment (ISE), will be used by advanced users. The PowerShell Console, a simple text interface that reminds of the Windows command line and even DOS 3.2 are the best way for beginners to use.

To start PowerShell as a Windows 10 administrator, click Start and scroll down the Windows PowerShell list of applications. Right-click the Windows PowerShell button on that line and choose Run as an Administrator. Search for Windows PowerShell in the Windows Server folder in Windows 8.1. In Win7, this is in the folder Accessories. You can run PowerShell as an "ordinary" user using the same series, but with a left-click. In any Windows version, you can check for PowerShell using Windows. With Windows 8.1 and Windows 10, you can insert it in the Power Menu of the Ctrl-X (right-click on a blank spot in the taskbar and select Properties, check the Replace Command Prompt box on the Navigation tab). It is a good idea to add PowerShell to your taskbar once you have it opened. Yeah, you'll like it so much.

Type old-fashioned Windows commands

You would be shocked how much Windows command-line syntax works in PowerShell as planned.

For instance, cd changes directories (such as folders) and you still list all the files and folders in the current folder.

You can start at c:\Windows\system32 or at c:\Users\<username >, depending on how you boot the PowerShell console. I use cd in the screenshot example. (Note space) move up one level at a time and then run dir in the directory C:\ to list all the files and subfolders.

Install the help files

Commands such as cd and dir are not native commands of PowerShell. They are aliases— replaces the actual commands of PowerShell. Aliases can be helpful for those of us with difficult to conquer finger memory. But they don't even start hitting PowerShell's most important parts.

Form aid followed by a command you know to get a feel for PowerShell itself. For example, I type help you in the screenshot.

PowerShell aid informs me that you are an alias for the Get-ChildItem PowerShell order. Sure enough, you can tell exactly what you saw with the dir command if you click the get-child item on the PS C:\ > prompt.

As mentioned at the bottom of the screenshot, PowerShell aid files are not automatically installed. To get it (you want it), in Administrator mode log on to PowerShell, then type update-help. It will take several minutes to install support files, and you may skip a few modules — Support for NetWNV and SecureBoot failed to install on my test machine. But when you are finished, the entire system of support is at your disposal.

From then, type get-help, followed by the PowerShell's "cmdlet," which you are concerned with and see all help for this item. For instance, the getting-help get-child item describes the childcare options. It also encourages you to enter variations on the subject. Therefore, the following:

get-help get-childitem -examples

Produces seven detailed examples of how the get-child item can be used. The PowerShell command get-child item documentation contains these seven examples and information on every available parameter for the get-child item cmdlet.

Get help on the parameters

You might have found in the Support dir screenshot that there are two listings under SYNTAX for babies. The fact that the cmdlet has two different syntaxes means that the cmdlet is handled in two ways. How do you distinguish the syntaxes— and what do the parameters mean? If you know the trick, the answer is easy. To get all info on the get-child item cmdlet parameters or any other cmdlet, use the the-full parameter, like this:

get-help get-childitem -full

It lists what you can do with the cmdlet and what can (or may not!) happen line by line. See screenshot. See screenshot.

By choosing the specifics of the parameter, you can somewhat see that get-child item can be used to retrieve "child" objects in a position that you define (including the names of the subfolders or filenames) with or without specific matches. For instance: get-childItem"*.txt"-recurse retrieves a list of all the"*.txt" files in the current directory, and all the subfolders (by parameter-recurse). Whereas, get-child item "HKLM:\Software" returns the list of HKEY LOCAL MACHINE\Software's high-level registry keys.

I'm sure you can see just how strong this kind of access needs to be if you have ever tried to get into the registry via a Windows command line or a batch file.

Nail down the names

There is a reason why our cmdlets look the same so far: get-child item, update-help, and get-help follow the same word-noun convention. Thankfully all cmdlets of PowerShell use this convention, with a verb before a (singular) noun. Those of you who spent weeks fighting for VB and VBA commands can breathe a sigh of relief.

Take a look at some of the most important cmdlets (thanks to Ed Wilson's Hey, Guy Scripting!). Begin with the cmdlets you enter and collect useful information, such as:

Set-location:

Sets the current workplace to a given location:

Gets the content of a file:

Copies copy-item files and folders:

Copies the item from one position to another remove-item:

Deletes the processing files and folders:

Get the processes running on a local or remote computer:

Gets services running in a local or remote computer invoke-web read;

To see how a particular cmdlet works, use get-help, as you can readily find out what the cmdlet needs in the help file. For example, if you want to copy all of your data and folders to c:\temp, you'll use: copy-item c:\users\[username] \Documents* c:\temp If you type a few nice keys in the PowerShell setting. PowerShell can fill in a copy element and space, for example, if you type copy-i and press the tab key. When you can't figure out a cmdlet and PowerShell, you will get a detailed explanation of what went wrong.

Try cmdlet. Use this cmdlet. If so, ignore it. Invoke-web request askwoody.com You get a shortlist of the content declarations, headers, images, links, and more. (You might attempt to set up a program to read the "about" box, if necessary) See how things work? See how? Notice that the invoke-web request cmdlet "returns set of forms, links, photos, or other essential HTML elements"— precisely what you should see on your computer.

Some cmdlets help you to monitor or groom PowerShell:

get-command:

get-verb: lists all the cmdlets that are available (this is a long list)

clear-host:

Diverse parameters (remember, get-help) allow you to narrow down the commands and the choices you might use. To see a list of all the cmdlets that function in conjunction with the Windows Services, try this, for example, get-command* -service. Here's the outcome:

Get-Service

New-Service

Restart-Service

Resume-Service

Set-Service

Start-Service

Stop-Service

Suspend-Service

You may combine these cmdlets in almost any section of PowerShell with other cmdlets. This is where the pipes come in.

Bring in the pipes

You know of the redirection and pipes if you have ever used the Windows command line or slogged via a batch file. Both the redirection (> character) and pipes (character) take the output from an operation and stick it elsewhere. For example, to filter exciting results, you can funnel the output of a dir command into a text file, or pipe the result of a ping command into a find.

dir> temp.txt
ping askwoody.com | find "packets" > temp2.txt

In the second above command, the search command searches for string packets in the piped output of a ping askwoody.com and sticks all lines that fit the temp2.txt file. Perhaps unexpectedly, PowerShell works fine with the first of these commands. You want something like this to run the second command:

ping askwoody.com | select-string packets | out-file temp2.txt

Using redirects and pipes dramatically increases the versatility of the Windows command-line: Instead of scrolling down the screen for a text string, for instance, you can create a piped Windows command that is screening for you.

PowerShell has the capacity for piping, but it's not limited to text. PowerShell then allows you to transfer an entire object from one cmdlet to the next, which is a "fact," which is a mixture of data (called properties) and the actions (methods) which can be used on the data.

But the hard part is the alignment of the objects. The type of object transmitted by one cmdlet must suit the kind of objects the receiving cmdlet accepts. Text is a very simple thing, so lining up items is easy if you're working with text. Other artifacts aren't so simple.

How can I work it out? Hello to the cmdlet. Welcome. If you want to know what type of object a cmdlet creates, pipe it in. When you try to find out what processes are running on your computer, for example, and limit the options to the cmdlet, this is how you find out what the cmdlet get-process produces:

get-process | get-member

The command generates an extensive list of the properties and methods for get-process, but you can see the type of object generated at the very beginning of the list:

TypeName: System.Diagnostics.Process

You have to find another cmdlet that operates with System. Diagnostics. The process as input to manipulate the performance of the get-process (as opposed to showing a long list of active methods on the monitor). You use to wait for a willing cmdlet. PowerShell:

get-command -Parametertype System.Diagnostics.Process

This lists all the cmdlets that System. Diagnostics. The process can manage.

Some cmdlets are known to take almost any form of input. First, among them: where-and-which. Perhaps confusingly, the objects run one by one across each element transmitted from the pipeline and apply whatever criteria of selection you request. A special marker called $ is available. That helps you to go one at a time through each object in the pipe.

Say you wanted to list all the processes running on your machine called "svchost" — you want to fit the Name property of svchost in PowerShell. Download this order PowerShell:

get-process | where-object {$_.Name -eq "svchost"}

The cmdlet where object looks at each System. Diagnostics. Process document compares the.name to "svchost;" if it fits, it spits out the end of the pipe and is type on your display.

POWERSHELL HISTORY

According to PowerShell, Microsoft device stacks management systems and network administrators had to use various tools, languages, and technologies to simplify and integrate. Administrators used batch files for some projects, which can be executed using Command Prompt (or DOS Shell, for those of you who still remember this term). Maybe Visual Basic Scripting Version (VBScript) has been used for other tasks. However, Windows Scripting Host (WSH) may have been used for additional tasks. The list continues.

Administrators had to be creative in many ways because they didn't have a single language and tool that they could use to connect different tasks with Microsoft (and not Microsoft). On the other hand, Unix and Linux administrators always had C-shell and comfortable dependency. At that time, Microsoft did not have a command-line tool that powerful.

In PowerShell. Join. This incorporation and automation prerequisite gave birth to PowerShell. PowerShell's founder, Jeffrey Snover, initially incubated PowerShell under the Monad project. Initially, he described Monad as the next-generation automation platform.

More than ten years later, PowerShell has already improved, matured, and become the platform for the automation and integration of Microsoft products (and even non-Microsoft packages).

By 2002, Microsoft began to develop a new approach to the management of control lines. It also included developing a new shell called Monad. The Monad Manifesto, a white paper written in 2002. The design of this shell and the ideas for a structured platform that utilizes the. The NET frame, through automation tasks, was included. Monad was first demonstrated at the 2003 Professional Developers Conference in Los Angeles. Microsoft has released the three beta versions of Monad on 17 June 2005, 11 September 2005 and 10 January 2006. In April of that year, Microsoft renamed Monad a Windows PowerShell to become a core component of the Windows operating system.

Since today, several Microsoft products have embraced PowerShell and supplied multiple cmdlets with their respective software installations (we shall discuss them later). Windows Server, Active Directory, Swap,

SharePoint, SQL Server support PowerShell, and support has expanded over the years.

Versions Of Powershell

PowerShell 1.0:

The Microsoft update for Windows Vista, Windows XP SP2, and Windows Server 2003 SP1 were released in November 2006, version 1.0. This version is an optional Windows Server 2008 component.

PowerShell 2.0:

Windows Server 2008 R2 and Windows 7 have been integrated with PowerShell version 2.0. It is launched with Service Pack 1, Windows Server 2003, Service Pack 2 for Windows Vista and Service Pack 3 for Windows XP.

This version contains improvements to the hosting API and the languages of scripting.

The new features of PowerShell 2.0 are as follows:

PowerShell remoting

Background jobs

Steppable pipeline.

Script Debugging

Windows PowerShell ISE (Integrated Scripting Environment)

Network file transfer

PowerShell 3.0:

Windows Server 2012 and Windows 8 are built with PowerShell version 3.0.

Microsoft released it with Service Pack 1, Windows 7 with Service Pack 1, and Windows Server 2008 R2 with Service Pack1 for Windows Server 2008.

This version is an internal component of the Windows Management Framework (WMF3) kit containing the WinRM remote support services.

The new features of PowerShell 3.0 are as follows:

Scheduled tasks

Session connectivity

Delegation support

Automatic Module Detection

Improved code Writing

Help update

New commands

PowerShell 4.0:

The Windows Server 2012 R2 and Windows 8.1 versions of PowerShell 4.0 are incorporated.

The Windows Server 2008 R2 SP1, Windows 7 SP1, and Windows Server 2012 are also available from Microsoft.

The following are the latest PowerShell 4.0 features:

Desired State Configuration (DSC)

A new default execution policy

Save-help

Enhanced debugging

Network diagnostics

PowerShell 5.0:

This version was released as an internal part of the Windows Management Framework (WMF 5.0) on the web on 24 February 2016.

The default version is Windows 10 and Windows Server 2012.

The new features of PowerShell 5.0 are as follows:

The Debugging for PowerShell

Context Jobs / Debugging for PowerShell

Runspaces in remote processes / the Resources, Methods, etc.·

PowerShell class descriptions / PowerShell class definitions (resources, methods)

PowerShell 5.1:

PowerShell 5.1 and the Windows 10 Anniversary update were released on 2 August 2016. The release is scheduled for 19 January 2017. Windows 7, Windows Server 2008, Windows Server 2008 R2, Windows 7, Windows Server 2012, and Windows Server 2012 R2 versions were available from Microsoft.

This is the first version of "Heart" and "Desktop" in two versions.

FEATURES OF POWERSHELL

Windows PowerShell is available in its fourth release when these lines are written, which comes with many improvements and enhancements. In this section, we concentrate on the key features that have a significant impact on the users of Windows PowerShell to understand the nature of PowerShell; then, we ensure that these features are covered alongside other features while we read this book.

Powershell Remoting

PowerShell Remoting is a native execution of Windows remote controls built on top of the Windows Remote Management protocol (WinRM). WinRM is supported by Windows Vista, Windows 7, Windows Server 2007, and Windows Server 2012, based on my super Google results.

The remote control feature enables PowerShell cmdlets to be executed on remote systems, which help to manage remote computers on a single machine. The remote execution function is based on WinRM technology. PowerShell Remote is like a Remote desktop session; you can disconnect your session from the same or a different machine without disconnecting any running program, application or script, and connect to that session from where you left off.

Enable powershell remoting

If you want to run Windows PowerShell computers remotely, you must first allow PowerShell remote control. You can then run PowerShell commands on the remote machine with the Invoke command and Enter-PSsession cmdlets.

On a local Enable-PSRemoting^ machine. You can log into this device locally or via Remote Desktop to allow PowerShell remote removal from a computer and then run enable-PSRemoteing on a PowerShell prompt with administrator rights. If the current PowerShell link type is set to the public, the above command generates a mistake message as PowerShell removal is allowed by default for private and domain connection types only.

Computers for the working group^. In the Active Directory setting, PowerShell removal works best. If you want to access workgroups or machines, you have to find a few additional settings.

If your network connection type is set to the public, the -SkipNetworkProfileCheck parameter, the PowerShell remote authentication relies on Active Directory. By default, PowerShell remote controls can only bind computers that are domain members. You must link the IP addresses of computers into the TrustedHosts in a working group environment. You must also ensure that the Windows Firewall is opened for Windows Remote Management on remote computers. Type "firewall" on the remote computer after you click Start and click Advanced Settings in the firewall Control Panel program. Right-click the Release Rules and pick the New Regulation. In the predefined region, select Windows Remote Management and then follow the wizard. To improve security, you should suggest using HTTPS in a working group setting rather than HTTP for PowerShell removal.

Only administrators can connect via PowerShell remote for non-administrators^. By default. If you want to allow a single non-administrator remote from PowerShell, you can link the account to the local user group Remote Management.

The Remote Management Group only exists on Windows 8 (or Windows Server 2012) and higher computers. To allow PowerShell remote operating by several non-administrator groups, you can set up a new Active Directory group (maybe "PowerShell Remoting") and add the corresponding domain users to that group. Then add the new domain group to the local remote management users group on all the machines whereby with the aid of group policy restricted groups, you want to allow PowerShell removal for these users.

Notice that this procedure only allows standard users to connect via PowerShell remote control. But they have administrative privileges similar to the rights on the computer.

With Group Policy^. To allow PowerShell to remotely on multiple computers, Group Policy can be used. Three polices are relevant: Enable WinRM, Set Automatic initialization of the WS management program, Allow Windows Firewall Remotion Management. If you have enabled an incoming Firewall Remote Administration exception on remote machines, you can automatically trigger the policy by right-clicking on the GPMC container icon and then clicking Group Policy Update. If not, computers must be restarted.

You can use Microsoft's free remote control tool, PsExec, to enable PowerShell remotely on a single machine. This choice helps if the remote desktop on the remote computer is not switched on.

PsExec requires, however, that ports in Windows Firewall for file and printer sharing or remote management are open. These ports can be opened via Group Policy: System Configuration > Management Templates > Network > Network Connections > Windows Firewall > Domain Profile. Additionally, you can also configure the Windows firewall with the aid of computer settings> Settings for windows > Security > Windows firewall with Advanced Protection. To allow PowerShell removal from PsExec, open a command prompt with Admin Rights in the folder you copied PsExec and

If you want to allow virtual remote control on a Hyper-V server, you can also use PowerShell Direct if your guest operating system is Windows 10, Windows Server 2016, or Windows Server 2019. PowerShell Direct^.

You can enter this command (.Enter-PSSession-ComputerName < hostname >) to test PowerShell remote remotes you have enabled. This opens up an interactive session with a remote system where you can enter commands for PowerShell executable on a remote machine. If you want to connect to a different account than the one you logged on a local computer.

Background Job

The idea of background jobs was introduced by Power Shell, which runs cmdlets and scripts asynchronously on local and remote devices without impacting the user or interacting with the console.

PowerShell code can be executed in two ways: synchronous or asynchronous.

You probably are thinking of synchronous execution when you think about a PowerShell script. This means that PowerShell runs code one line at a time in the script. It begins one command, waits for completion, and then starts another. Every line is waiting for the one to end.

This is great for small scripts and scripts that rely on the line to complete before it is executed, but it doesn't have to be designed like that most of the time. This is merely easier at the cost of results. You have other options when creating a script that could take many minutes or even hours. Alternatively, a term called jobs can be used to execute code asynchronously. Through PowerShell, work is a piece of code in the background. The code begins but returns control immediately to PowerShell so that another code continues to be processed. Job performance is great, and a script does not depend on previous code execution results.

As an example, I may have a script that works on a bunch of remote servers. Each action is unique because one server's action doesn't rely on another server's action. Let's say we've got a script that checks whether a server is online first. If so, a folder is formed and a few text files added to that folder. The work is meaningless.

As-is, this script runs the Test-Connection command on a server and generates a folder and text file if it is accessible on the server. This will be done by one server, then by another, then by another. Let us say you point to 100 servers, and half of them hang on Test Connection, and for some reason, they are extremely slow. It'll take you to run this script forever. Let's see how context work can be done.

To create a simple background job, we use the Start-Job command using a parameter called ScriptBlock that contains the code that we want to execute.

Note that an entity with a bunch of properties is returned instead of returning the hostname. The job is going on. By using Get-Job, I can check the status of the job and determine the ID. The state is complete so that I can check the results now. I use the Receive-Job command to see what output the background job generated. To simplify things, I can transfer the Get-Job output directly to the Receive-Job to inspect the output.

Scheduled Job

A scheduled job looks like a background job; both jobs run asynchronously without interrupting the user interface, but the difference is that a background job needs to be started manually. Scheduled work can, however, create the background work and schedule it for later performance using some cmdlets instead of using the Task Scheduler wizard manually. You can also access the results of scheduled work and resume lost jobs.

Scheduled jobs are batch jobs created and managed with PowerShell as background tasks. The expected jobs on the surface look, function, and sound much like an old pattern of Windows: scheduled tasks. The similitude between the two instruments also confuses people. Planned jobs and scheduled tasks are, for the most part, the same but apply to different applications. Microsoft has designed scheduled jobs to be precisely identical to scheduled jobs so that you do not have to learn a new scheduling syntax.

Creating a Scheduled Job

We will build our first scheduled job before we get too far ahead of ourselves.

This scheduled function updates the support files on the local computer automatically. I've got this on every machine I work on, and it means I'm never concerned about losing support or it's out of date elsewhere.

If you jumped right into the workstation and tried to run this example, you probably only knew about registering a new scheduled job: you must do so in a higher PowerShell session. That is, make sure you run PowerShell first as "Administrator." Throughout the next few posts, we will cover each part in more detail, but we will quickly cover each line in the series.

The New-ScheduledJobOption command defines options that relate to the Task Scheduler. These are optional, but they can be avoided by paying attention to them.

The first choice we choose suggests that we want to run the "Administrator" job in PowerShell, which is beneficial as you have high privileges to update system-wide support files.

The second option means that if the workstation has no network connection, the function will not work. With Update-Help downloading new help files from the web, there's no point running if there isn't a connection to it.

First, New-JobTrigger determines when the job is going to start. Strictly speaking, you don't have to provide a trigger, so that your job only runs if you trigger it manually. I have tried to list the parameters that can be read by humans: "run each day at 1 AM." The final order documents our planned activity in the task planner. In this way, we provide the previously defined options and triggers and also give the job a name and give the code, in the form of a script block, the task to execute.

Steppable Pipeline

This allows script blocks to be separated into a separate stage pipeline. It helps you to call the script block's beginning, phase, and end methods to ease execution sequence control.

Why the powershell Pipeline Rocks!

Leaving the PowerShell pipeline and regularly switching to foreach instead is certainly not a panacea and a universal remedy. The PowerShell pipeline was designed for one reason: it is a significant alternative to foreach loops. Both have cases of their use:

Downloading: foreach works like downloading a video: you have first to fit all the data you want to memory. It can eat a great deal of memory. And since Vorach can not start working until the input data is complete, you may not see any results for a while. It's really like watching a video: you need a lot of storage when you download it, and you need to wait until you download the whole file until you can see it. Each is better if you have the data collected in a variable already.

Streaming: The forecharging object and pipeline work like streaming a video: you can already watch it while the video is downloaded and does not need to store the video anywhere. All you need is the memory to store the current photo. That is why many people think the pipeline is quicker because the initial results are shown quickly. The advance object is easier to save time and process the data directly from an upstream cmdlet to give the user fast feedback.

Script Debugging

You can set breakpoints on rows, columns, functions, variables, and commands, as in Visual Studio. You can also specify actions to be executed when the interruption is hit. Step-in, over and out of functions, are also supported; even a call stack can be provided. Visual Studio also allows the debugging of script languages such as VBScript or JScript at the source level. This is implemented internally using the same process model on which managed application debugging depends. One of the reasons why the CLR used the debugging model in practice when it was first released to the public in 2002 was that script debugging had been using it effectively since the mid-1990s. In both cases, the debugger needs the collaboration of the script host or CLR execution engine to support the debugging of the target process at the source level.

How script debugging works

It is helpful first to explain a few basic concepts of how to script languages are run in Windows to understand how to script debugging works. The Active Scripting specification is the key to this architecture. In the 90s, Microsoft implemented this specification and specifies a set of COM interfaces for hosting scripting languages in any compatible host program. For Windows, both VBScript and JScript are Effective Scripting languages, which are fully implemented according to the specifications. The Active Scripting specification defines a language processing engine and uses the Active Scripting host when interpreting the script. The vbscript.dll and jscript.dll, both with Windows in the system32 directory, are examples of active scripting engines. Types of Active Scripting hosts include the webserver (server scripts embedded in ASP or ASP.NET pages), internet explorers (client scripts hosting in web pages), and Windows scripting hosts (cscript.exe or wscript.exe) which ship with Windows. They can be used to host command prompted scripts. There are also Active

Scripting engines from third parties that support other script languages, such as Perl and PowerShell.

The Active Scripting specifications also specify a contract (several COM interfaces, again) for debuggers to use the host. A smart host is called Active Scripting host that supports debugging (that is, implements the required COM interfaces). All recent releases of Internet Explorer, IIS, and the Windows scripting hosts are smart hosts that implement such interfaces, which are essential to the magic of Visual Studio debugging scripts that are hosted by any such method. The Visual Studio debugger ships a process debugger (PDM) part (pdm.dll) to insulate script engines from the ability to debug a file. The PDM component usually has the same purpose as the CLR debugger thread and mscordbi.dll serve during managed debugging. One way that Active Scripting debugging is not managed code debugging is because smart hosts usually do not expose their debugging services defaults while a debugger thread is always on managed code with the CLR. For instance, you have to allow script debugging first with Internet Explorer by clearing the Disable Script debugging option in the Tools\Internet Options\Advanced tab. In the same way, if you want to debug scripts on Windows scripting hosts using /X, you need to explicitly enable debugging scripts in the Windows script host system (cscript.exe/wscript.exe). There is also a UI option for server-side debugging for the IIS Web Server Manager.

Error-Handling

Powershell offers an error-handling mechanism using the Try{}, Catch{}, and, lastly, as in.. NET languages,{} statements. PowerShell has several different kinds of errors and may occasionally be a bit of a minefield. Two aspects must also always be taken into account: how you write code that causes errors and how you deal with those errors in your code. Let's look at some ways to efficiently use and manage the various types of errors that you can encounter in PowerShell.

Different types of errors

Terminating Errors

Finishing errors are usually an "exactly what it sounds like" kit. It is very similar to C #'s Exception method, but PowerShell uses its base error object ErrorRecord. Its standard features are the following:

Trigger trying/catching blocks

Caller return power, with the exception, if not done using the attempt/catch block.

Non-Terminating Errors

Non-terminating errors are the concession of PowerShell demanded that it be a pipeline-friendly shell. Not all mistakes warrant halting all current activities and need only warn the user that a small error has occurred, but the remaining items continue to be processed.

About non- termination errors, non-termination errors:

Do not cause attempt/catch blocks.

Do not affect the control flow of the document.

Method for handling errors

cmdlet Preferences

Through PowerShell, all cmdlets have ubiquitous parameters. These include ErrorAction and ErrorVariable, which specify how cmdlets manage non-end-out errors. ErrorAction determines how a cmdlet operates when a non-end-out mistake is found. In the example above, ErrorAction is defined as SilentlyContinue, which means the cmdlet is not running if a non-terminating error occurs. The ErrorVariable parameter determines the name of the variable for the error object, which was caused by a non-extinct error. ErrorVariable is defined as Err, as shown in the previous example. Notice that the variable name has no $prefix. However, you use the variable name with a $prefix ($Err) to access ErrorVariable outside a cmdlet. Also, the resulting variable is valid for the current PowerShell session or associated script block after defining ErrorVariable. This means that other cmdlets will connect error objects with the + prefix to an established ErrorVariable.

Trapping Errors

If the terminating error occurs, the default behavior of PowerShell is to show the error and interrupt the execution of the command or script. To use custom error management instead fix an error, you have to specify an exception trap manager to stop the termination error (ErrorRecord) being sent to the default error management system. The same applies to non-termination errors because the default behavior of PowerShell is to show the error and keep running the command or script. ExceptionType is the first element, which defines the error type that a trap recognizes. If no ExceptionType is specified, all errors are accepted.

The code element may consist of a command or collection of commands, which are sent to the trap after a mistake has been made. The concept of trap commands is optional. The last part, Keyword, decides whether the trap causes the statement block to proceed or terminate where the error occurred.

Break—This causes the exception to be rethrown and stops the current scope from executing

Continue—It allows the current scope execution to continue at the next line where the exception occurred

Return [argument]—Stops the current range from running and returns the argument, if specified

The trap uses the keyword Return [argument] if a keyword is not specified, and the argument is the ErrorRecord that was first delivered to the trap.

The throw keyword

You can create your termination errors in PowerShell. This does not mean that the wrong syntax is used to create errors. Instead, you can intentionally create a termination error by using the thrower keyword, as shown in the next example, when you try to run the MyParam.ps1 script, a user can not identify the MyParam parameter claim. This type of behavior is very useful when data from functions, cmdlets, data sources, programs, etc. is not what is expected, so the script or collection of commands can not execute properly in the execution phase.

Tab Expansion

Tab expansion is an automatic execution that completes the cmdlets, properties, and parameter names once by pressing the tab key.

Command-line shells often provide a way to automatically fill in the names of large files or commands, speed command entry, and provide hints. PowerShell lets you complete file names and cmdlet names with a Tab key. To automatically fill out a filename or path from the option, type the name and press Tab key. PowerShell will extend the name automatically to the first match it finds. Pressing the Tab key will loop through all the available options repeatedly. The cmdlet name tab extension is slightly different. Type the whole first part of the name (the verb) and its corresponding hyphen to use the tab extension on a cmdlet name. You can complete more of the partial match term. For example, if you type get-co and press the Tab key, PowerShell automatically expands this to cmdlet (note that it also changes the case of letters as standard). Pressing the Tab key again replaces PowerShell by the only other equivalent cmdlet name, Get-Content.

Better tab completion with psreadline

I could never get the default tab completion handle of PowerShell and saw it drive people away from PowerShell. Fortunately, you don't have to stick to the default implementation.

You can configure a project called PSReadline to add read-style tab completions to your shell. Just issue this command: Set-PSReadlineKeyHandler -Key Tab-Function Complete, Unfortunately, it's not as fast as Bash in macOS, but it's much more user-friendly than default setup. Attach it to your profile to fire it every time you open PowerShell. You can get PowerShell to tell where you want to do this by sending this command: echo profile Create this file in your favorite text editor.

Constrained Runspaces

This allows the development of PowerShell run spaces with a set of restrictions that include the access and execution of scripts, cmdlets, and language elements. You may wish to limit the Windows PowerShell command available for your host application for purposes of performance or protection. To do this, build an empty System. Manager. Automation. Runspaces. InitialsessionStatus by calling the System. Management. Automation. Runspaces. Initial session. Build* process.

The use of space to load only the commands you assign improves performance dramatically.

You use System. Management. Automation. Runspaces. Sessionstatecmdletentry to configure cmdlets for the initial state of the session.

You can also take private orders. The host application, but not the user of the application, may use private commands.

Windows Powershell Web Access

In Windows Server 2012, the PowerShell console launched a Web-based version. Here, we can run PowerShell cmdlets from any web browser that is not accessible on desktops, tablets, or mobile devices as well. In Windows Server 2012, Microsoft Windows PowerShell Web Access is a feature that acts as a Windows PowerShell Portal, offering a console-like PowerShell display in a browser for cmdlets or scripting, to connect to a remote computer. The web browser must support JavaScript and cookies.

The application does not require additional management software or browser plug-ins. Windows PWA is not included in Windows Internet Explorer only and can be used on other Web browsers, such as Safari, Google Chrome, and Firefox. Windows PWA does not include Windows InternetExplorer.

Since PowerShell Web Access (abbreviated as PSWA) has been available for years, I'm not going to get into too many specifics about the installation and configuration of your app. But, I'll talk briefly about how you can and can't use it.

To begin with, any browser can be used to connect to your internal PSWA endpoint or the outside world. Internet Explorer is going to do just fine, not that you should necessarily use them, but versions as old as IE 8.0. The majority of mobile apps are good, too, as long as JavaScript is supported. The balance of the loose needs is, as you can imagine, a "not so snappy" GUI. This shows how much attention Microsoft has given to this feature in recent years since I am using a Windows Server 2019 box, even though the Windows Server 2016 web page says. Cosmetics, once you log on to the PSWA page, you end up on a terminal window, and you can start editing cmdlets. PSWA uses remote controls to link to a particular machine; therefore, when logging in, the device name parameter is needed. When you've connected to the PowerShell console, as the $PSVersionTable performance demonstrates, you can do more than just run cmdlets. For example, the current server version/construction can be shown. NET classes and methods such as the System. Environment class and its OSVersion property. Console programs like ipconfig can also be named. Support for tab completion and execution history and most other PowerShell features, you know. Finding and installing modules via the PowerShellGet module exposed cmdlets is an example, given that you are connected to a PowerShell-version device. The MSOnline module can be downloaded easily if it is not already present. You can connect to Office 365 and start user management once the module is installed.

Requirements for running windows powershell web access

To run the portal, Windows PowerShell Web Access includes the Web Server (IIS),.NET System 4.5, and Windows PowerShell 3.0 or Windows PowerShell 4.0. You can use either Add Roles, and Features Wizard in Server

Management or Windows PowerShell Deployed cmdlets for Server Manager to install Windows PowerShell Web Access on a server running Windows Server 2012 R2 or Windows Server 2012. When using the Server Manager or its deployment cmdlets, you install Windows PowerShell Web Access, and you automatically update your positions and features as part of the installation process.

Windows PowerShell Web Access enables remote users to use Windows PowerShell in their Web browsers to access the organization's computers. While it is a convenient and efficient management tool, Windows PowerShell Web Access poses security risks and should be configured as safely as possible. We recommend that Windows PowerShell Web Access administrators use security layers, including cmdlet-based authorization rules with Windows PowerShell web access, and security layers available in Web Server (IIS) and third-party applications. This guide includes both unsafe examples recommended only for test environments and examples recommended for secure deployments.

Network File Transfer

This function provides the native support for priority, asynchronous file transfers between machines through BITS (Background Intelligent Transfer Service). A network file transfer (NFT) is the mechanism by which files or data are received or transmitted through a local or global network (such as the internet) through a native network transmitting protocol. There are several methods and protocols used for network sharing of data, such as HTTP and FTP over the internet, as well as Ethernet for small networks and local area networks. If a node receives the file, it is called downloading, while when the file is sent to another node or server, it is uploaded.

A network file transfer is initiated in two different ways: when the receiver begins the download or transfer, the transfer on the push is initiated by the sender. The transmission speed is determined primarily by the network's capacity and, to a lesser extent, by the protocol capacities used.

A transfer of network files over the network can happen transparently, for example, if a node communicates with a different node without being actively notified of the transfer or explicitly, for example, when a user requests a particular website via HTTP or downloads a file via FTP. It is the protocol that defines the transfer convention, which provides a structure for the transfer between two endpoints, such as how to send bits from the file and other metadata such as filename, size, time tag, and any headers required for the transfer to be successfully initiated or completed.

Transactions

This Windows PowerShell feature allows us to start a transaction, indicate which command is a component of the transaction, and either roll-back or commit a transaction. The start-transaction cmdlet starts a transaction, which is a set of commands handled as an entity. You can complete or execute a transaction. Instead, it can be completely undone or rolled back to the original state of any data changed by the transaction. Since the commands are handled as a unit in a contract, all commands are either transferred, or all commands are rolled back.

Default, if an error is caused by a command in the transaction, transactions are automatically rolled back. You can modify this action using the RollbackPreference parameter.

The cmdlets used in a transaction will help transactions. Cmdlets supporting transactions have a parameter for

UseTransaction. The provider must facilitate transactions to perform transactions in a system. The Windows PowerShell Registry Provider supported transactions in Windows Vista and later versions of the Windows OS. You may also use Microsoft. PowerShell. Commands. Management. TransactedString to include terms in any Windows system version that supports Windows PowerShell transactions. Many providers of Windows PowerShell may also support transactions. Just one account can be active at a time. If a separate, independent transaction is performed during the transaction in progress, the new transaction becomes an active transaction and the new transaction must be completed or roll-back before making any changes to the original transaction.

HOW TO LAUNCH POWERSHELL

Many IT professionals use PowerShell to manage computers and devices on Windows and perform all kinds of administrative tasks. You need to know how to start it before you can use PowerShell. Therefore, we have made a long list of all available methods, including admin rights, to start this tool. Read on and see all of them:

Start PowerShell using search (all Windows versions)
In Windows 10, the quest is one of the fastest ways to open PowerShell. Find PowerShell in the search field from the taskbar. Then click or tap the Windows PowerShell result. If you want to run PowerShell as the administrator, right-click on the search results for PowerShell, (or tap and hold if you use a touchscreen), and then click or tap the "Run as administrator." If you use Windows7, open the Start menu.
If you want to run PowerShell as an administrator, right-click on the result of your Windows PowerShell quest and choose "Run as Administrator." Then press Enter on your keyboard when the search results are shown or click Windows PowerShell results.

For PowerShell to be run as an administrator, right-click on the PowerShell search result of Windows, and in the menu shown, pick "Run as administrator."

Start the PowerShell using the Run window (all Windows versions)

One of the fastest ways to start PowerShell is to use the Run window in any modern version of Windows. One quick way to open this window is to click your keyboard's Win+R keys. Enter or select Yes, type PowerShell, and press Enter.

Launch the PowerShell from the Start Menu (in Windows 10 and Windows 7) or the Start Screen (in Windows 8.1)

Open the Start menu in Windows10 and go to the Windows PowerShell shortcut tab. You can find the Windows PowerShell shortcut here. Begin the PowerShell from the Start menu (in Windows 10 and Windows 7) or from the Start screen (in Windows 8.1). Open the start menu for Windows 10 and go to the Windows PowerShell shortcut tab. There you can find a Windows PowerShell shortcut.

Go to the Start screen in Windows 8.1. Open the Apps View and scroll right until the Windows System folder is open. Click or tap on the shortcut to Windows PowerShell. NOTE: Right-click the PowerShell shortcut to run it as an administrator, and then click "Run as Administrator."

Run PowerShell using its executable file (all Windows versions)

File Explorer (Windows 10 and Windows 8.1) or Windows Explorer (Windows 7) may also be enabled. If you're using Windows 32-bit, go to: "C:\Windows\System32\WindowsPowerShell\v1.0\." You'll find the 32-bit powershell.exe file there.

You should browse to: "C:\Windows\SysWOW64\WindowsPowerShell\v1.0\ "if you have a 64-bit version of Windows.

NOTE: If you don't know if your Windows is 32 or 64-bit, read this tutorial: Which version of Windows is available for me? To run the file as admin, right-click powershell.exe and then select the option "Run as administrator."

Start PowerShell using the WinX power user menu (Windows 10 only)

Windows 10 features a hidden power user menu called WinX. The easiest way to start is to press the Win + X key on your keyboard, but you can also hit the left-hand corner of your screen with a right-click (or hold) on the Windows logo. Here are shortcuts to launch PowerShell, both with restricted permissions and administrative rights.

You prefer to use the Windows PowerShell shortcut to start it.

Create a shortcut for PowerShell on your desktop (all Windows versions)

If you want to use shortcuts, do not hesitate to build a PowerShell shortcut. If you don't know how to create shortcuts and need help, read this guide: how to create shortcuts for Windows application, file, folder, and a Web page. Only keep in mind that you type PowerShell as the position of the element to which you are building the shortcut.

The path to the powershell.exe file can also be used, provided by the fourth method of this guide.

Use Task Manager to start PowerShell (all Windows versions)

The Task Manager is another way to open PowerShell. Launch Task Manager: Pressing the Ctrl + Shift + Esc on your keyboard is a fast way. Click or tap "More Details" on the Task Manager when you're using either Windows 10 or Windows 8.1 and open the File menu in its compact mode. Click or tap "Run New Task," then in all Windows versions, open a File menu and click or tap "Run New Task."

Open PowerShell by using the shortcut from our collection (all Windows versions)

We also created a comprehensive collection of Windows shortcuts. Download, uninstall, and you can find the Windows PowerShell shortcut for your Windows version in the Windows PowerShell sub-folder.

Open PowerShell from the Command Prompt (all Windows versions)

An effective geeky method involves starting PowerShell from the Prompt command. If you opened the Prompt button, type "start PowerShell" (no quotation marks), and press would Enter on your keyboard.

If you want to start PowerShell as an administrator from the Command Prompt, then make sure you open the Command Prompt as an administrator first.

POWERSHELL CMDLET

The PowerShell commands are based on cmdlets. When designing PowerShell cmdlets, Microsoft made many design strategies. Firstly, the ability to scan cmdlet names or make them at least easy to find. Also, PowerShell commands or cmdlets are designed with a consistent syntax, rendering them accessible from the command line or for creating powerful scripts. As in the Get-Service, the Stop-Service, or the Import-CSV format, cmdlets use the Verb-Noun. The verb portion of the name of the cmdlet shows the action to be taken on a noun. Cmdlets that are used to request information usually use the Get verb, as with Get-Process or Get-Content. Commands used to modify something typically start with the verb Set, whereas those adding a new entity often start with Add or New. In many instances, these verb-noun combinations can be estimated or predicted due to the standard naming convention.

The only feature of PowerShell intended to boost the usability of the command line is not standardized cmdlet naming. Standard names are also used for parameters typically used in PowerShell. One example is-

ComputerName, which enables a cmdlet to be run on one or more remote computers. Similarly -Credential is used to provide the user's login credentials with a credential object to execute the command as a specific user. Windows PowerShell has for years been a popular scripting language among Microsoft IT professionals, and for a good reason. PowerShell's strength over other languages is the simplicity and readability that enables inexperienced scripters and users to learn it easily. By contrast, PowerShell uses thousands of cmdlets in new Windows operating systems (currently Windows 10 and Windows Server 2019). Mostly, these cmdlets can do virtually anything on a Windows computer via a graphical user interface.

Sometimes the sheer number will make it hard for beginners to find out where to start. Of course, cmdlets are often used, not to mention cmdlets to simplify the learning of PowerShell.

Specialized classes within NET are PowerShell cmdlets (commands). One of the more confusing aspects of PowerShell, which users of other languages must understand is that everything in PowerShell is an object, and these objects have properties (properties are object data, such as a file name) and methods (object operations such as deleting a file). You can't use PowerShell or think of it as the "Windows Bash" because PowerShell isn't operating like Bash. In comparison to Bash that uses text streams, PowerShell automatically constructs several input data as objects.

Get-Help

The Get-Help cmdlet may well be the most valuable PowerShell cmdlet because it allows the user to see what a particular cmdlet is doing, the cmdlet parameters, and the best example of how the cmdlet is used. You can see it as similar to the Linux man command. Get-Help shows more knowledge than just cmdlets, and you can learn about things like operators and language concepts.

The –Name parameter is used in this first example to display the help in the Cmdlet Add-Content. Also, the — Full parameter is used to show the entire help page in this topic, which contains a synopsis, parameter explanations, and examples. In fact, for several developers, it is sufficient to view examples of how a cmdlet is used, so the — Examples parameter is used instead of specifying —Full. The definition is prefixed with about to see these topics in Get-Help. For example, the PowerShell command would be about Comparison Operators to view information about the concept of comparison operators. One helpful trick when you want to find a keyword in Get-Help is to use wildcards in the name parameter, which returns the subject name.

PS C:\> (Get-Help -Name *operators*).Name

about_Arithmetic_Operators

about_Assignment_Operators

about_Comparison_Operators

about_Logical_Operators

about_Operators

about_Type_Operators

Get-Command

In PowerShell, a module is a group of useful cmdlets, such as the ActiveDirectory module, that interact with Active Directory. The Get-Command is used to view cmdlets from PowerShell modules built on your local computer or your current PowerShell session. Similar to Get-Help, Get-Command's not a cmdlet, but it's very helpful when trying to fix a problem while you are in a shell.

For example, Get-Command will display each cmdlet installed in modules and snapins locally. This alone is not very beneficial, because the performance is important.

A useful feature of Get-Command is the ability to locate the cmdlets in a given module. This is particularly useful when you first know what a module can do. The –Module parameter is used for this purpose, and the module name is shown in the PackageManagement module below.

PS C:\> Get-Command -Module PackageManagement
CommandType Name

----------- ----

Cmdlet Find-Package

Cmdlet Find-PackageProvider

Cmdlet Get-Package

Cmdlet Get-PackageProvider

Cmdlet Get-PackageSource

Cmdlet Import-PackageProvider

Cmdlet Install-Package

Cmdlet Install-PackageProvider

Cmdlet Register-PackageSource

Cmdlet Save-Package

Cmdlet Set-PackageSource

Cmdlet Uninstall-Package

Cmdlet Unregister-PackageSource

Get-ChildItem

The Get-ChildItem cmdlet (both in Windows PowerShell and PowerShell Core) is an alias for the dir command in PowerShell. Therefore, if used on a file system, it lists objects inside the folder as you do. This feature is nice because it works with PowerShell providers outside of a file system, including the Windows registry, environment variables, variables, and customer providers such as a VMware datastore. In the test folder, children's things are displayed and contain three text files. The next command will pip output to Where-Object and pick only elements with the text1.txt tag. Note that Where-Object is a cmdlet used in PowerShell for filtering objects based on specific values. As previously mentioned, Get-ChildItem interacts with the Windows registry. This example uses Get-ChildItem to show the NoAutoUpdate registry key value on Windows, a key that deactivates automatic Windows updates. Please note that the pipe character") ("can be used for the PowerShell console multiline commands.

```
PS C:\> Get-ChildItem $RegKey |
>> Get-ItemProperty -Name NoAutoUpdate |
>> Select-Object -Property NoAutoUpdate
```

NoAutoUpdate

0

Foreach-Object

Forward loops are necessary for any language of programming, and PowerShell is no exception. This cmdlet only executes a function in a group of objects for each object. The Foreach-Object cmdlet is used to process objects from version 3 of PowerShell with two different approaches. One approach is to use brackets with a script block. The other approach is to call a property or method directly. Both of these approaches are shown. The -Process parameter is used in the first example to print the Name property to the console. In the second example, the member parameter is used without a block file. The foreach expression can be used in a PowerShell script without providing pipeline input. Remember that this is not the same thing as the cmdlet of the Foreach-Object. The forecast requires a variable and the collection that will be emphasized by PowerShell. The variable changes for each object in the set in the script block.

The variable in this snippet is $item. Whenever the $collection variable is iterated, $item changes its value. In this case, it is first the test1 string and then the test2 shifts.

```
$collection = 'test1','test'
foreach ($item in $collection){
  Write-Output $Item
}
```

Get-Member

PowerShell is all about objects since almost everything is described as an entity in PowerShell. Whereas Get-Help and Get-Command provide useful information in PowerShell on cmdlets and principles, Get-Member shows the information on the properties and methods of a given object. The test folder is put in a $test variable. Next, the cmdlet Get-Member shows the properties of the folder object. Such knowledge is very helpful because it allows you an idea of the properties PowerShell can use to a folder. For example, the FullName property coincides with the full directory path, and the Creation Time property corresponds to the time the folder was generated on the file system. The $test variable is cycled by pressing the tab key, which changes through methods and properties to see the CreationTime property's value.

PS C:\> $test.CreationTime
Monday, October 17, 2016 3:23:39 PM

Managing Files And Folders

Regardless of your IT industry niche, you may be able to manage your files and folders in some way as part of your daily grind. Whether it transfers directories to other server locations, archives log files, or searching for large files; almost every system manager spends part of his day handling files and folders. When repeated tasks in multiple files or the same set of tasks are repeatedly performed, PowerShell automation can save you real-time.

Finding files and folders The dir command was one of the first methods the managers used to understand in computer time. For new players, dir will list the files and folders in the directory you specified. PowerShell is fitted with a similar command as the Get-ChildItem cmdlet. Get-ChildItem helps you to quickly build a directory listing of files so that you can then use either a piped command for these files or allocate the output to a variable. Get-

ChildItem can be used by entering a route through the pipeline, using a the-Path parameter, or following the name of the cmdlet immediately. It is important to check those parameters made available by the cmdlet to change the answer returned by Get-ChildItem. Parameter-Filter is one way to search for data. The Get-ChildItem cmdlet returns only direct children in the target directory by default. A the-recurse switch can be used to extend this feature to retrieve lists within the current tab. With PowerShell 4.0 Get-ChildItem, you can limit the output by using the –File or the Directory switch to either a file or folder. Previous versions of PowerShell were required to pipe the result to Where-Object and to filter on the PSIsContainer property. Here is an example of both approaches for returning the directories in C: Users:

Get-ChildItem C:Users -Directory Get-ChildItem C:Users | Where-Object {$_.PSIsContainer –eq $true}

The-Force switch must be used to discover hidden or system files. Get-ChildItem can also be used with the -Hidden, -ReadOnly, and –System switches in and above to retrieve only those files that are secret, read-only, or system data. In previous versions, the same features can be accomplished by filtering on the mode property with Where-Object:

Get-ChildItem C:Users | Where-Object {$_.Mode -like '*R*'}

Checking if a file exists

Sometimes all we need to ask is if a file exists or the folder path is correct when dealing with data. PowerShell offers a cmdlet for this test-path validation, which returns either a true or false value.

As a precautionary measure before trying to copy or remove a specific file, Test-Path is often useful.

Copying, moving, and deleting files

PowerShell is willing, as you would assume, to perform standard file operations in a single pass on multiple objects. You can copy a file or more files from one path, as defined by the-Path parameter, to the location set in the -Destination option by using a cmdlet copy-item.

Similarly, the cmdlet Move-Item is used to move a file or folder. The-Recurse switch should be used when a folder

86

structure is copied or transferred, to have the cmdlet act on the folder and its contents. In some cases, a the-Force switch is necessary, for instance, when a read-only file is overwritten by copying.

The Delete-Item cmdlet will delete files and folders. As is the case with many cmdlets, a the-Force option should be used when a secret or read-only files are detected, and-Recurse should be used for removing the folder and its contents.

Using PowerShell -WhatIf and -Confirm

Scripts have been said to allow people to do stupid things exceptionally quickly. Use the -WhatIf option for most cmdlets discussed here before you pull up the trigger on a broad delete process.

The -WhatIf option helps you to see what happens if you execute the script or instruction without the possible adverse effects of removing critical business details. It should also be noted that -What is not limited to file operations, it is commonly used across PowerShell.

For scripts that you want to run manually or worse, you need to run a subordinate manually. It helps you to need user interaction in advance of the project. This is often best just as long as everything is ready to go (full file backup, replication disabled, etc.) before large files are started.

Objects, piping, filtering and more

The trick for PowerShell is that many of the cmdlets are object-oriented in addition to the structured naming and other features that make it intuitive. When dealing with objects, it is simple for PowerShell to alter multiple items with a single line of code, make changes in thousands or use the objects to collect data or perform actions on other similar objects. PowerShell objects Objects refer to artifacts that contain several attributes or properties, such as character strings, information lists, and numerical values for those not familiar with the terminology. A good example of an object is a Windows process, which is found with the Get-Process cmdlet and includes many characteristics indicating the executable name, the priority, the CPU usage, and the memory use. Get-Member not only will show you the properties of an object and the data types it holds, but it will also give you the kind of object, which can then be used to find other cmdlets that support the type of object.

Piping

PowerShell lets you use a technique known as piping to lift cmdlets and objects. You can quickly and easily pick items using the pipe character) (and then act on them. A perfect example of piping is to kill certain processes using java stop process. Also, you can restart services on a single line like a Get-Service Spooler Restart-Service.

Cmdlets with the same noun are often used for piping, but the procedure is not limited to cmdlets with the same language. You can find other cmdlets that can be used to obtain a piped command using the object form returned by Get-Member. The cmdlet Get-Command with the type of object defined using-ParameterType gives a cmdlet list that accepts the specified type of object.

Filtering

There is a complete list of PowerShell cmdlets used for the heavy lifting of objects, in particular the object noun. Many of the cmdlets are one of the most common cmdlets, while others are used for specialized tasks. The cmdlet Where-Object helps you to restrict or filter the object to which the pipeline passes—the Get-Service Where-Object{$.DependentServices -ne$null} command, for

89

instance, would return a list of services with dependencies. The syntax used with Where-Object is noteworthy and also applies to some of the other objects. In PowerShell, the squiggly brackets are used to delineate a code block, indicating, in this case, the state of the pipeline. The automatic $ variable indicates the current instance of the evaluated object. PowerShell comparison operators use hyphenated formatting; so-eq (equals) is used to find the exact correspondence with the term "stop." Using aliases can save time and effort to use the PowerShell console interactively. The cmdlet Where-Object uses the question mark?). PowerShell 3.0 will make the Where-Object syntax even simpler by eliminating from the pipeline the need for the script block, and the automatic variable. This command in PowerShell 3.0 is the same as the command above Get-Service? $null $dependentServices.

Acting on objects

ForEach object is used to act on each object case. ForEach-Object is quite like Where-Object from a syntax viewpoint, with both the script-block and the default variables used in both cmdlets. Where ForEach-Object excels, tasks are too complex for simple piping against each object instance.

You may have to list file protection in a file-sharing, for example, in which case you can use the pipe of the Get-ChildItem cmdlet to ForEach-Object and use the Get-ACL file security list for the file list with a full-name parameter ($.FullName).

As with Where-Object, cmdlet for each object can be simplified by alias with the% sign (percent). The PowerShell 3.0 syntax is also provided for even more intuitive use.

It is a good idea when filtering an object or carrying out an action on object instances to avoid Where-Object and ForEach-Object where possible. Most cmdlets provide an a-Filter option or other parameters, which can help to limit the number of results without having to look at each object, usually leading to a substantial improvement in performance.

Likewise, ForEach-Object works on each instance of the piped object. When possible, items should be directly piped to cmdlets that can perform the required action for the whole object, without having to list each element in the object.

Comparison Operators And Conditional Logic

System administrators decide daily on many criteria which maintenance tasks to perform on servers. Repeated administrative tasks are often automated with PowerShell by using logic to replicate this process of decision-making. Various techniques for achieving the desired results can be applied using comparisons, filters, and conditional logic.

PowerShell comparison operators

You won't get too far to create PowerShell scripts without the conditional logic that starts with the comparison of values. The ability to test whether there is a user, whether a file was made, or if a device may link to another user requires a comparison with a value. The one big gotcha in PowerShell is related to syntax:-lt and-gt are used for comparisons rather than using the conventional comparison operators such as < or > PowerShell.

More generally, numerical values are used by most operators of reference, although they also have their position when they are dealing with dates or version numbers and other variables. The following table lists the most widely used reference operators.

CMDLET VS COMMAND

The IBM 8086 cutter from the floppy brought you back in the day to a green text screen with a cursor blinking at the familiar C:\ > prompt. My first exposure to programming was to get boot.ini and config.sys to run my games.

Finally, this C:\ > has been replaced by a good GUI and a harddisk boot. The command prompt (CMD) has been in existence for decades. Recently, CMD got an update, or substitution, with PowerShell, the Microsoft shell program for Windows 7.CMD was good for a long time, but PowerShell is like going straight from steam engines into battery autonomous cars.

PowerShell vs. CMD is like comparing kumquats to apples. Given the belief that the' dir' command acts in both interfaces, they are quite different.

PowerShell uses cmdlets that are autonomous programming objects that represent underlying management options in Windows. Until PowerShell, sysadmins were navigating the GUI to find such solutions, so that the process through clicking on the menus could not be reused to alter large-scale choices.

PowerShell uses cmdlet pipes to chain input and output data, like Bash in Linux, in the same way as other shells. Pipes allow users to create complicated scripts that transmit parameters and data between cmdlets. Users can develop reusable scripts to automate or change mass with variable data–for instance, a list of servers.

One of PowerShell's (many) nice features is the ability to create aliases for cmdlets. Aliases allow a user to create their names for different cmdlets or scripts, which makes switching between various shells simpler for a user:' ls' is a Linux bash command that shows directory objects like' dir.' Through PowerShell, the' ls' and' dir' are alias to' Get-ChildItem,' a cmdlet. As already stated, cmd is an ancient tool never intended for remote system management. Additional utilities such as Microsoft Sysinternals PsExec are needed to extend its functionality.

On the other hand, PowerShell offers many cmdlets to simplify the tasks of system management. It facilitates automation of various tasks, such as management of Active Directories, management of users and permissions, and the extraction of security configuration data. Also, PowerShell supports Linux now.

There are several reasons why Windows PowerShell replaced the default command prompt on Windows 10 and was preinstalled beginning with Windows XP. However, when using cmd, you don't need to feel the urgent need to turn to PowerShell. Many cmd commands work well in the PowerShell environment. In essence, Microsoft wanted system administrators to simplify their lives, and it created prompt aliases in PowerShell to help it interpret the old DOS commands as new PowerShell commands. All you can do with cmd is also possible with PowerShell, and often it is more convenient since there is a special environment where scripts can be developed and tested. Also, PowerShell is a live language with a strong community that is ready and ready to support the new users in the scripting of scripts. The explanation is that it just has more strength. One of the main differences is that PowerShell uses cmdlets instead of commands. Cmdlets put registry management and Windows management tools within users ' administrative scope. Command Prompt, by comparison, is limited to much simpler commands. There is a crossover between the two systems as PowerShell accepts commands prompt like ipconfigtocd. However, they are not classified as cmdlets but as aliases. Another important difference is that PowerShell focuses on objects. Every cmdlet data output is an object instead of a document. This facilitates the user's navigation through complex data. The use of the. The NET framework also enables the use of.NET interfaces through PowerShell scripts. In short, PowerShell is the steroid command prompt.

Loading up powershell

You must first access the main GUI before we discuss the fundamentals of PowerShell. You will already have access to PowerShell 5 if you're a Windows 10 user. Windows 8-8.1 users have access to PowerShell 4, but you will need to install it under.NET when you are on Windows 7. PowerShell provides two distinct interfaces across all operating systems.

The more advanced is the Integrated Scripting Environment, a complete Interface for experienced users. The basic option is the PowerShell console, which provides the user with a command line to enter their commands. Beginners will stick with the latter before they know PowerShell's basics.

You need to be an administrator to launch PowerShell on Windows 10. Sign in, press Start, and scroll through your apps as an administrator before you find Windows PowerShell. Right-click and choose Run as admin. Check for PowerShell in your device folder on Windows 8.1. In the same way, the default PowerShell directory on Windows 7 is the Accessories folder after the software has been installed.

How to run cmdlets

In short, a cmdlet is a command with a single function. As with a typical command or utility, you insert cmdlets in the command line. The primary way to communicate with the CLI is by cmdlets. In PowerShell, most cmdlets are written in C #and provide instructions for executing a function returning a. NET entity.

Within PowerShell, more than 200 cmdlets can be used. The prompt command for Windows PowerShell is not case-sensitive so that the commands can be typed in upper or lower instances.

The following are the significant cmdlets:

Get position-Get the existing

Set-Location directory-get the current

Transfer-item directory-move a file to a new location

Copy-item copy a file to a new location

Rename–a new file

Creating a new file

Use the Get-Command cmdlet for a complete list of commands available to you. You must type the following in the command line:

PS C:\> Get-Command

It is important to note that Microsoft prevents users in their default settings from using custom PowerShell cmdlets. You need to modify the Execution Policy from Restricted to RemoteSigned to use PowerShell cmdlets. Remote signed allows you to execute your scripts, but stops other users with unsigned scripts.

To change your RemoteSigned execution policy, type the command: PS C:\> Set-EXECUTION Policy. Type the command: PS C:\> Set-EXECUTION Policy - EXECUTIONPOLITICУ RemoteSigned. Make sure you have permission to set a new executance policy on your Administrator account.

Overlap with Windows Commands

When you're new to PowerShell, you should try and learn a whole new command library. Nevertheless, the terminology used on Windows command-line overlap with PowerShell is not understood by most new users. The fact that PowerShell is not case sensitive makes this easier.

Similar to Command Prompt, the cd command still switches directories on PowerShell, and you still list your files within the selected directory. As such, it is important to remember that you don't necessarily start at all. It includes helping to lower the learning curve you face with PowerShell and decrease the number of new commands you need to master.

It is important to note that these commands are not considered to be full PowerShell commands as aliases (Windows prompt command name of Powershell). So although in PowerShell you can use some of the Command Prompt commands, you will know as much about the new commands as possible. However, Command Prompt experience will definitely help new users to catch PowerShell and hit the ground.

HOW TO RESOLVE "OVERLAP: DUPLICATE OWNERSHIP FOR DIRECTORY" ERROR IN WINDOWS

Run DISM with the external media

First things first. Users who experienced this error used SFC or DISM mainly to inspect a system error that occurred on Windows 10 suddenly. Today, as you probably know, DISM (Deployment Image and Service Management) is the tool used by the command line.

Mostly, there are two ways to run DISM. The first approach is to replace broken system files with system resources (Windows Update included). The second relies on external sources to correct the mistake.

If, as seems to be the case with this situation, the first option fails, you can turn to the alternative and go it. You do, of course, have to build a bootable Windows 10 installation media to do this. Whether it's a USB stick or an ISO DVD. Once you have it, take the steps below to run DISM, which you have plugged in:

Install your installation media for Windows 10, be USB or ISO DVD. Right, click Start and open Command Prompt (Admin).

In the command line, type the following command and press Enter

If there's not any single error, enter this command and press Enter:

DISM/online /Cleanup-Image /ScanHealth

If DISM finds any errors, enter the following commands, and tap Enter:

DISM /Online /Cleanup-Image /RestoreHealth /Source: repairSourceinstall.wim

Don't forget to replace the "repair source" with the path to the installation media.

After the process is complete, restart your PC and check for changes.

In case, this fails, you continue with the alternative steps.

Run an in-place upgrade

Now, before we move to clean re-install, let us try using an on-site update to fix the system error. Namely, the system error instigator is most of the DLL file corrupted or deleted. Now in the event, the DISM scanning is short, we can always renew the current Windows shell using the installation media. In this way, the missing files are retrieved, and you should be wrongly clear.

The most feasible way to get the media is to use the Media Building Tool. This tool is important for Windows 10, so be sure to get it here. Make sure you pick the correct version, language, and architecture of Windows 10. It must look like your current version of the system.

For Windows Media Creation Tool, physical or virtual (mounted) installation drive, there are few ways to do this. We have ensured that you clarify everything you need to know, so follow the instructions carefully:

Plugin, install it on a hard drive, or just run the Windows Media Creation Tool.

Open the contents of both physical and virtual drives and double-click Setup.

Click on' Upgrade this PC now' and then Next, to accept the terms.

Click the "Download and install updates (recommended)" button after setup loads and then click Next.

Click Install once all updates have been purchased.

Choose to save your files and apps and click Next.

Wait until Windows 10 is' reinstalled,' run SFC / DISM again and check for modifications.

Reset this PC

Another more enjoyable solution you should consider is one of the newly added Windows recovery options. This is "Reset this PC" option, of course, that emulates the Factory reset from handheld devices. This option allows users to restore the device to factory values while retaining unchanged files and installed applications.

It is better than System Restore as it gives you a brand new system with intact files, settings, and applications. System Restore can not address the files that have been deleted from DLL.

Clean reinstall Windows

Ultimately, if neither of the previously advised approaches helped you resolve the problem, we can only suggest the reinstallation of a clean program. By starting entirely from scratch, you will indeed lose all your system partition settings and applications. Nonetheless, on the other hand, the sluggish complexities of updating to Windows 10 over older versions have been highlighted more than a few times. This is where the majority of problems begin, and clean reinstallation will deal entirely with them.

Follow the instructions for reinstalling Windows on bootable media (USB or ISO DVD):

Backup your device partition info.

USB plug-in or mount a Windows installation DVD.

Restart and enter the boot screen on your Mac. Choose the activation media to boot.

Wait until the files are loaded and click Download now.

Choose favorite settings and customize the build.

Label and pick system partition for installation.

Your PC restarts many times, and you should then look at the brand new and faultless Windows.

.

POWERSHELL DATA TYPES

So far, we have only worked with two types of data: strings and integer (or, more accurately, 32-bit integer). PowerShell supports many other types of information, such as floating points, strings, and boolean values. You do not have to specify specifically the data type of a variable; when initializing this variable, PowerShell automatically selects the data type you want — that is, the first time you assign a value.

In some instances, however, PowerShell does not use the data form you wish to use, as the example below shows:

$Number = Read-Host "Please enter a number"

$Square=$Number*$Number

Write-Host "The square of the number $Number is $Square."

If you didn't sleep in math class, it should be a bit surprising that this calculation results. PowerShell mistakenly assumed that the $Number variable's data type is String. As* is overloaded (the operator's execution depends upon the arguments), the program's second line multiplies a string instead of a number.

The second argument of an operator* must always be a number, so that PowerShell transforms the $Number data form into Int32 automatically. The first statement may, however, also be a set. As a consequence, PowerShell determines the value of "2"*2, which is 22" (2 "string is repeated twice).

In addition to assigning a data type automatically when you initialize the variable, PowerShell can also adjust the data type when the original data type does not fit into the operation. In the example above, PowerShell needs an operator number*; because the string "2" looks a lot like the number, it only converts it to integer 2.

Nevertheless, PowerShell can trigger an error if there is no reasonable way to convert the data type automatically, and the data type does not match the operation. For example, the following lines produce the "Can not convert value' b' in the system. Int32' error message." It is important to bear in mind that the automatic conversion does not alter the data type of the variable. Although the $b variable value in the example is used as an integer in the calculation, the data type remains String. You can use the GetType) (method to determine the type of variable.

If it surprises you that the variable has a process, you will have to wait for a follow-up post to discover the secret behind the above instruction.

We do not need to rely on the ability of PowerShell to convert data types automatically if we tell the interpreter we expect a number. This ensures our script functions as intended.

```
[Int]$Number = Read-Host "Please enter a number"
$Square=$Number*$Number
Write-Host "The square of the number $Number is $Square."
```

In the above code snippet, we explicitly declared the number Int32 (integer) by putting the type name before the variable name into quadrangles. A variable is considered "weakly typed," if its data type is only implicitly declared by assigning a value of a given kind. Defining the variable type in your script, specifically types the variable. As mentioned above, defining variable types explicitly will avoid undesirable outcomes in your scripts and make them more accurate. This is not the only reason why working with strongly typed variables makes sense. The things that you can do with a variable's value also depend on its data type.

You can, for example, save a certain date in a String data type variable and use the DateTime data type for that purpose. As long as you only want to display the date, the type of data you use doesn't differ. Nevertheless, you must declare this attribute as DateTime if you wish to use it in calculations.

Let us presume that you have imported log file dates and you want to know how many days have passed between a date and today: [DateTime]$Date = "February 28, 2015"

$Days = ($Today - $Date).Ds
Write-Host "The hacker encrypted all your servers $Days day(s) ago."

If you ignore the data type declaration in the above case, PowerShell politically tells you in a red-colored message that something went wrong: "Several undefined surplus loads for"

Below is a list of some commonly used data types:

Data Type Name

Description

[Array]

Array

[Bool]

Value is TRUE or FALSE

[DateTime]

Date and time

[Guid]

Globally unique 32-byte identifier

[HashTable]

Hash table, collection of key-value pairs

[Int32], [Int]

32-bit integers

[PsObject]

PowerShell object

[Regex]

Regular expression

[ScriptBlock]

PowerShell script block

[Single], [Float]

Floating point number

[String]

String

[Switch]

PowerShell switch parameter

[TimeSpan]

Time interval

[XmlDocument]

XML document

Hide File Extensions In Powershell Tab Completion

To check which file types Windows considers to be executable you can type $Env:PathExt.

PS > $Env:PathExt

.COM;.EXE;.BAT;.CMD;.VBS;.VBE;.JS;.JSE;.WSF;.WSH;.MSC;.PY;.PYW;.CPL

Similarly, you can type $Env:Path to get a list of places that Windows will look for files to execute by default.

PS > $Env:PATH

C:\Program Files\Docker\Docker\Resources\bin;C:\PowerShell35\Scripts\;C:\PowerShell35\;C:\Windows\system32;C:\Windows;C:\Windows\System32\Wbem;C:\Windows\System32\WindowsPowerShell\v1.0\;C:\Program Files (x86)\NVIDIA Co ram Files\nodejs\;C:\Program Files\Git\cmd;C:\Program Files

(x86)\Skype\Phone\;C:\Users\jmreicha\AppData\Local\Mic
rosoft\WindowsApps;C:\Users\jmreicha\AppData\Local\at
om\bin;C:\Users\jmreicha\AppData\Roaming\npm

However, the issue is that, when you start typing in an extension that is part of this course, say "PowerShell" and add the file extension to the executable by Windows. Since I have a more relaxed* nix type shell, the file extensions have to be treated annoyingly.

Below I'll give you a hack to mask this request from you. It is much more work than I thought to add this behavior, but we can add it with some support from some people. We must overwrite the Powershell default tab completion functionality with our own, and afterward, we must load this override into the Powershell prompt via a custom file Profile.ps1.

To make this work, the first step is to look after the default tab.

ScriptBlock This will scatter the code that handles the tab completion actions. To achieve our customary behavior, we have to circumvent the original code with our reasoning (I wish I came up with this myself, but unfortunately). Notice the entire code, only the custom logic. The full script is shown below.

```
$field                                           =
[System.Management.Automation.CompletionResult].GetF
ield('completionText', 'Instance, NonPublic')
$source.CompletionMatches | % {
    If    ($_.ResultType    -eq    'Command'    -and
[io.file]::Exists($_.ToolTip)) {
        $field.SetValue($_,
[io.path]::GetFileNameWithoutExtension($_.CompletionTe
xt))
    }
}
Return $source
```

The code looks a little bit bullish, but it just checks to see whether the command is executable and on our device route and if it just eliminates the extension.

To get all this running, we need to create a logic file and read it by Powershell at load time. Go ahead and paste a code such as no ext tabs.ps1 into a file. I put it in the Powershell path but can put it anywhere (~/Documents / WindowsPowerShell).

Whenever you start a new Powershell session, if you want to hide the extensions, we need to create a new Powershell

Profile and load our script (more information on creating Powershell Profiles here when you're interested). You can skip this step if you already have a custom profile.

New item $profile file form-force After creating the profile, proceed to edit it with the following setting.

#Not ext tabs source to remove file extensions from path executables.

C:\Users\jmreicha\Documents\WindowsPowerShell\no ext tabs.ps1 Open and open your shell again, so you can't see the extensions for your file any longer.

There is one last little tidbit I have found, but it was very useful and worth sharing with other Powershell N00bs.

PowerShell 3 and above offers some nice key bindings to hop around the CLI, like a shell based on a bash if you know or have a history on* nix systems.SPECIAL VARIABLES

Variables are the key part of the PowerShell Windows. In the PowerShell variables, we can store all types of values. For example, we can store the outcome of commands and the elements used in paths, names, settings, and values: the specific objects, Microsoft. NET Framework objects are stored.

A variable is a memory unit that stores the data. The variable name begins with the dollars) ($sign in Windows PowerShell, such as $process, $a. The variables ' names are not case-sensitive and contain spaces and special characters. By default, the value of all the PowerShell variables is $null. A variable in computer science (and incidental computing) is a memory location containing arbitrary information for later use. In other words, it's a temporary container in which data can be stored and data collected. This can be either a word (a string in programming lingo) or an integer in the Bash shell. Text data can only be stored in most shells in a variable. Data stored in variables can be almost anything in advanced shells and programming languages, from strings to sequences to objects.

Similarly, variables in PowerShell can be almost anything. You need to use a prefix for defining a PowerShell variable, which helps to identify the aliases, cmdlets, filenames, and other things a shell operator may want to use. Every combination of alphanumeric characters (A–Z, and 0–9) and the underscore) (characters are case-sensitive. You may never (knowingly) used a variable before on your screen, but in another area of your life, you possibly used a variable. You use grammatical variables when you say things like "give me this" or "look at this" (then you talk about them as pronouns). The importance of this, and this depends on what you think of or what you say as an indication for your audience to know what you mean. If you do arithmetic, you use unknown values by using variables, even if you possibly do not name them.

This addresses PowerShell variables that are running on Windows, Linux, or Mac.

NOTE: The PowerShell session on Linux open-source operating system is the examples given in this chapter so that if you're on Windows or Mac, the file paths differ. Nonetheless, Windows automatically converts / to\, and every example works across all platforms, as long as you remove clear differences (for example, your username is statistically improbable).

What are variables for?

Whether in PowerShell, you need variables depends on what you do in a terminal. For some users, variables are a vital means of data management, while for others, they might be minor or temporary, or they may not exist for some.

Variables are a device. You can use them if you find a use or leave them alone to know that your operating system handles them. Nevertheless, knowledge is power, and knowing how variables function in Bash can lead to all kinds of unexpected creative problems.

Set A Variable

To create a variable, you do not need special permissions. You are free to create, use, and typically harmless. You construct a variable in PowerShell by specifying a variable's name and then using the Set-Variable command to set its value. An example below creates a new variable called FOO and sets its value to the string $HOME / Documents: PS > Set-Charge-Charge -Set-Variable -Name FOO-Value "$HOME / Documents" With the Get-Variable (GV for short), you can see the effects for yourself. You can also cover the variable in quotations to ensure that it is read correctly, as you have described it. It protects any particular characters that may exist in the variable, but that does not matter in this case, but it is still a good habit of forming:

PS> Get-Variable "FOO" -valueOnly

/home/seth/Documents

Note that the FOO content is not exactly what you set. The vector literal string was $HOME / Documents, but it now appears as/home / Seth / Documents. This is because you can nest variables. The $HOME variable indicated whether in C:\Users on Windows,/home on Linux, or /Users on Mac the current user home directory. Because $HOME has been integrated into FOO, this variable is expanded if it is remembered. This helps you to write portable scripts that operate across platforms by using default variables.

Variables are usually intended to transmit information between systems. Your variable is not very useful in this simple example, but it can still communicate information. For instance, since the content of the FOO variable is a file path, FOO can also be used as a shortcut to its value reference directory.

To refer to the contents of the variable FOO, not the variable itself, preset a dollar sign) ($to the variable:

PS> pwd

/home/seth

PS> cd "$FOO"

PS> pwd

/home/seth/Documents

Clear A Variable

A variable can be removed with the command Remove-Variable:

PS> Remove-Variable -Name "FOO"

PS> gv "FOO"

gv : Cannot find a variable with the name 'FOO'.

[...]

In practice, it is not usually necessary to remove a variable. Variables are relatively "cheap," so when you don't need them, you can create them and forget them. Nonetheless, you may want to ensure that a variable is empty so that unnecessary information is not transmitted to another entity that can read the variable.

Create A New Variable With Collision Protection

For PowerShell variables, the behavior is slightly different than in other shell settings. We will see that uniquely, PowerShell handles everything as an object variable. In PowerShell, variables are memory units where we store values. Variables began with the symbol $and followed by a letters string like:

$this_is_a_variable

The letter string should be continuous, and I would advise you, as a best practice to use concise names of variables, to use a camel case combination, where each term is capitalized, or each function is separated by an underliner as shown above.

PowerShell variables are not case-sensitive and may contain any particular letter, number, and character.

Sometimes, you may have reason to think that you or some other process have already set a variable. If it is not overridden, you can either use New-Variable that is designed to fail if there already exists a variable with the same name, or use a conditional statement to the first search for a variable:

PS> New-Variable -Name FOO -Value "example"
New-Variable: There is already a variable called' FOO.'
Note: Assume that FOO is set to/home / Seth / Documents in these instances.
Additionally, you can create a simple if statement to validate an existing variable:
PS> if ($FOO)

```
>>{ gv FOO } else
>>{ Set-Variable -Name "FOO" -Value "quux" }
```

Add to a variable

You should add an existing variable instead of overwriting it. Variables have different types in PowerShell, including string, integer, and array. If you decide to create a variable with more than one value, you must choose whether you need a string or an array with a specific character. One way or the other, you may not care, but the application receiving the information on the variable may expect one way or the other.

Use the+= syntax to add data to a string variable:
```
PS> gv FOO
foo
PS> $FOO += ",bar"
PS> gv FOO
foo,bar
PS> $FOO.getType().Name
String
```
Arrays are particular types of PowerShell variables and need an array from ArrayList. This is not possible in this

article because it requires a more in-depth analysis of the internals of PowerShell. NET.

Go Global With Environment Variables

So far, the variables created in this chapter are local, which means they only refer to the PowerShell session in which you create them. You should create environment variables, which will be covered in the future, to create variables accessible to other processes.

Types Of Variables

You can store any object type, including integers, strings, arrays, and hash tables, in a variable. And objects representing processes, services, logs of events, and computers. PowerShell variables are dynamically typed, so they are not limited to a single object category. A single variable may even contain a set or array of various object types simultaneously.

You can use an attribute class and cast notes to ensure that a variable can only contain certain object types or objects that can be converted to that type. PowerShell tries to convert the value to its type if you seek to assign a value of another kind. The assignment statement fails if the type can not be converted.

To use cast notation, enter the name of a type with brackets (on the left of the declaration of assignment) before the variable name. This example generates a variable of $number that can only be an integer, a variable of $words that can only contain strings, and a variable of $dates that can contain only DateTime objects.

The various variables in the Windows PowerShell are as follows:

User-Created.
For Intelligent Variables.
See Variables of Choice.

User-created Variables

The variables that the user creates and maintains are called variables created by the user. The variables we generate on the PowerShell command-line only exist when the PowerShell window is open. The variables are also removed when the PowerShell window is closed. The variables in the script can be created with the local, global, or script scope.

Automatic Variables

The variables that store the PowerShell state are called automatic variables. PowerShell generates this type of the variable, and its values are modified by PowerShell to ensure its accuracy. The consumer can not change these variables ' values.

Preference Variables

Preference variables are those variables that store the Windows PowerShell user preferences. This type of variable is generated by the Windows PowerShell and is compiled with default values. Any consumer can change the value of the variables of choice.

Using Variables In Commands And Expressions

Type the name of a variable, followed by the dollar sign), ($to use a variable in a command or expression.

If the name of the variable and the sign of the dollar are not included in quotation marks, the variable's value is used in the command or expression.

If the variable name and dollar symbol are included in a single quotation mark('), the expression uses the variable name.

See about Quoting Rules for more information on using quotation marks in PowerShell.

The value of this example is the PowerShell console PowerShell user profile path of the $PROFILE variable.

Variable Scopes

The variable scope of PowerShell is significant; scopes determine where the variable is available. A power shell variable is available in the scope and child scope, except when you declare the variable private or global. As with any other shell that allows scripting, most modern language scripting variables will have the scope. The scope is where the attribute is for use in parts of a session or document. PowerShell has the following scopes:

$global–Variables are accessible in the current session to scripts, functions, and any cmdlet.

$script–Variables are only accessible within the running script context and are discarded after the script has finished running.

$private–Variables are only available for either a script or method in the current scope. They can not be moved to other regions.

$local–Variables are only true in the framework of the existing script or session. Each scope named by you can read the contents of a variable, but not modify, and this is the default when a variable is created.

Automatic Variables

When the session is running, automatic variables are generated and populated. These variables will include user information, system information, default variables, time variables, and PowerShell settings. To see variables and what they do, either we can do Get-Help about Automatic Variables or list them and select only the name and description of their variables. One of the variables that you can find is to see if the last cmdlet you called runs successfully or not if the exit state is saved in? With a value that is False if it failed and True if it succeeded. When executing the variable system with the last exit code, it would be $lastexitcode to return the error exit code found during execution, or0 if completed successfully. Some of the automatic variables can be modified to customize the session, others will be read-only, and some will be modified with the sel sel session. Many of these variables are useful when working with PowerShell, so I ask you to read the help of automatic variables.

Exploring Automatic and Preference Variables
PowerShell offers the variable: drive that allows you to control the PowerShell session variables. The variable:

drive is like a file system drive (e.g., C), except that variables are accessed instead of file system objects. For instance, this command lists all the variables in your session: Get-ChildItem Variable: You will see a list of variables and their values while running this command. Initially, these are all automated variables (which store something about the status of PowerShell) and preferences (which store PowerShell user preferences). The values of the automatic variables can not be changed, but the values of the choice variables may be changed.

Automatic variables tell you about the current state of PowerShell. For instance, the $PWD automatic variable contains the current location of PowerShell.

The $PWD variable contains an entity, and its Path property is returned to the first order. The value is C:\ at this point. The following command uses the cmdlet Set-Location to change the current location to the drive variable: Remember that the $PWD variable path property automatically reflects the adjustment (hence the automatic term). For verification only, the third command retrieves the value of the Path property of the $PWD variable, this time variable:\. The last command returns the current position to the C drive.

Preference variables allow you to change a PowerShell user preference. One of the frequently reported preferences is $ErrorActionPreference, which will enable you to configure how PowerShell responds to ineffective errors. $ErrorActionPreference is set to Continue, meaning that PowerShell will emit the non-termination error, and the cmdlet will continue to function. (non-termination errors don't prevent cmdlet from continuing). Sometimes you might want the cmdlet stop when an error occurs, in which case you should run the command:

$ErrorActionPreference = "Stop"

Many times, you may not care about non-terminating errors, so with this order, you want to remove them altogether:

$ErrorActionPreference = "SilentlyContinue"

Note that the $ErrorActionPreference variable is the same as the cmdlet parameter-ErrorAction. The difference is that the cmdlet parameter-ErrorAction affects just one cmdlet, while the variable $ErrorActionPreference affects all cmdlets.

Exploring Environment Variables

PowerShell provides an Env: drive that allows you to control variables of the system. In PowerShell, the parenting process (i.e., the program which started the current PowerShell session) copies the environment variables. The initial values of the environmental variables are usually the same as in the Control Panel. (Your profile script may adjust the initial value of environmental variables with PowerShell in order not to suit the values of the Control Panel, but it goes beyond the reach of this discussion.) You may start the command: Get-ChildItem Env: this means running the Set command in Cmd.exe to view all environment variables in the current PowerShell session.

In Cmd.exe, a string of percent (e.g., percent ALLUSERSPROFILE) is available that tells Cmd.exe to replace the name with its value. The percent of characters are not used by PowerShell to get the values of environmental variables. You can control the value of an environment variable in two ways in PowerShell. First, you can access it directly from the Env: drive using the $Env: name syntax, where name is the name of the environment variable. For example, to find out the ALLUSERSPROFILE value, you would execute the command.

$Env:ALLUSERSPROFILE

That C:\ProgramData returns. Alternatively, the Get-Item cmdlet can be used to retrieve the Env: drive value from the environment variable. You are, in this case, not using the $symbol, as shown here: Get-Item Env: ALLUSERSPROFILE The first syntax ($Env: name) is most common and works in double-quoted strings when using variable interpolation. For example, the "ALLUSERSPROFILE is $Env: ALLUSERSPROFILE" command returns C:\ProgramData is the ALLUSERSPROFILE variable.

Getting Help with Variables

The PowerShell Help system provides a lot of variables information. The following support topics are suggested to you: about Variables, over Automatic Variables, over Preference Variables, and Environment Variables. You can read these help topics online by following this syntax: help theme, where you want to see the subject. For instance, if you want to read the topic about Variables, you will run the command: help over Variables if you run PowerShell 3.0, you will need to download first the aid topics and get an error message when attempting to view the aid topic. To do this, start PowerShell as an administrator with a right-click on the PowerShell shortcut icon and select Run as an admin. Type the command: Update-Help The device must be able to download the help topics on the PowerShell prompt.

Understanding Aliases

Sadly, a lot of typing needs to be done with PowerShell before you run a script. PS C:\ > get-process where-object{ $.company -match".*Microsoft*"} format-table name, ID, Path–Autosize This is a long command to type: for instance, open a PowerShell console and try to type the following commands. Fortunately, as with most shells, PowerShell supports cmdlet and executable aliases. So, you can use the default aliases of PowerShell if you want to decrease typing in this order. The Get-Process example looks like this with these aliases: PS C:\ > GPS? $.Company-match".*Microsoft *"} FT Name, ID, Route–

AutoSize This is not a significant decrease in typing, but alias save time and prevent typos. Use the Get-Alias cmdlet, as shown in the following example, to obtain a list of currently supported PowerShell aliases in your session. Please note that the example shows only a small subset of the PowerShell aliases available because of space limitations; the list is returned when you execute Get-Alias cmdlet.

PS   C:\>   get-aliasCommandType   Name Definition----------- ----   ----------Alias   ac Add-ContentAlias   asnp   Add-PSSnapinAlias clc   Clear-ContentAlias   cli   Clear-ItemAlias   clp   Clear-ItemPropertyAlias clv   Clear-VariableAlias   cpi   Copy-ItemPS C:\>

Discovering Alias Cmdlets

Several cmdlets of aliases allow you to define new aliases, export aliases, import aliases, and display existing aliases. You can get a list of all the relevant alias cmdlets by using the following command:

```
PS  C:\> get-command  *-AliasCommandType      Name
Definition----------- ----       ----------Cmdlet       Export-
Alias   Export-Alias [-Path] <String...Cmdlet        Get-Alias
Get-Alias [[-Name] <String[]...Cmdlet        Import-Alias
Import-Alias  [-Path]  <String...Cmdlet             New-Alias
New-Alias  [-Name]  <String>  [...Cmdlet             Set-Alias
Set-Alias [-Name] <String> [...
```

You already saw how to use Get-Alias cmdlet in the current PowerShell session to create a list of aliases. Export-Alias and Import-Alias are used to export and import alias lists from a PowerShell session to a separate one. Finally, the cmdlet of New-Alias and Set-Alias enables the current PowerShell session to define new aliases.

Note-The PowerShell alias implementation is tight. As previously mentioned, an alias only works for cmdlets or executables, not for executables with a parameter. There are, however, ways to overcome this constraint. The command in a variable is specified by one method, and then the variable from other commands is called. The problem here is that in the current PowerShell session, the variable can only be called unless it is specified in the.ps1-

profile. The second method (preferred) is to insert your command into a task.

Creating Persistent Aliases

When using the New Alias and Set-Alias cmdlets, the aliases created are valid only in the current PowerShell session. If a PowerShell session exits, all previous aliases are discarded. To manage the aliases through PowerShell sessions, you must define them as shown in this example in your profile.ps1 file: set-alias new object set-alias time.

While command shortening is desirable, it is not recommended to expand the use of aliases. One explanation is that aliases to scripts aren't very portable. For instance, if you're using multiple aliases in a script, at the start of the script, you're needed to include a Set-Aliases sequence to ensure the aliases are present, regardless of the computer or session profile when the script is running.

Nevertheless, the major concern is that aliases can often confuse or distort the true meaning of commands or scripts. The aliases you identify may be important for you, but not everyone follows your logic with aliases. If you want other people to understand your files, too many aliases must be used. See, instead, how reusable functions are developed.

POWERSHELL SCRIPTS

PowerShell is based on script processes and commands. Once we have the structure for making our scripts, we can incorporate loops and conditions into some of the more advanced logic.

PowerShell scripts are just text files with the special ps1 extension filename. To build a script, enter in a new Notepad file a bunch of PowerShell commands (or you can use a text editor you want), then save the PowerShell file with NAME.ps1, where the NAME is a nice summary of your script-no room, of course.

You can enter a PowerShell window to run a PowerShell script you already have.

Of course, a script must do more than one thing, or you don't need a script. Scripts are already popular in IT; for years, administrators use login scripts to regularly customize desktops and environments of users every time a user logs in. Since technology has been enhanced, you can almost script all–from the bare metal installation on a server to the server loads, including the installation of Exchange and file server functions. We won't go that further into this piece, but for our purposes, the basic idea behind a text is to do two or three things and finish. The first is the changeable element. The second is the script factor that works on all things. Let's look at every step.

Creating Your First Script

Most of the commands included in this chapter are interactive, which means that the PowerShell prompt enters commands and returns the output. While the interactive use of PowerShell is useful for tasks only once, it is not an efficient way of carrying out routine automation tasks. Fortunately, PowerShell can read files containing stored commands that allow a sequence of commands to be written, saved, and retrieved when needed. These command sequences are commonly known as scripts.

PowerShell scripts are text files that are stored with a.ps1 extension. You can make a text file with commands which compose a PowerShell script with any text editor (e.g., Notepad). For instance, open Notepad and write the following command: get-service where-object{ $Status-eq "Stop"} Next, save this file in a directory of your choosing with the ListStoppedServices.ps1 name. The C:\Scripts list is used for this example.

You need to change the execution policy of PowerShell before you can run this script because the default setting does not permit running scripts to avoid malicious scripts. You use the Set-ExecutionPolicy cmdlet to adjust this setting, as shown in the following example. You may also use Get-ExecutionPolicy cmdlet to check PS C:\ > RemoteSignedPS C:\ > get-ExecutionPolicyRemoteSignedPS C:\ > The RemoteSigned Policy allows script development to run on the spot without digitally signing, but still needs the digital signature of scripts downloaded from the site. These settings will enable you to run unsigned scripts on your local machine but protect unsigned external scripts.

After changing PowerShells RemoteSigned execution policy, you can type in the entire directory path and filename of the script in any PowerShell session. This output is generated by entering C:\Scripts\ListStoppedServices.ps1. Although the basic one-line script is simple, it still illustrates how to write a script and use it in PowerShell. If required, you can include more commands to carry out the automation function. An example is the following:

```
param ([string] $StartsWith)$StopServices = get-service |
where-object {$_.Status -eq "Stopped"}write-host "The
following $StartsWith services are stopped on" ´
"$Env:COMPUTERNAME:"          -Foregroundcolor
Yellow$StopServices | where-object {$_.Name -like
$StartsWith} | ´ format-table Name, DisplayName
```

The script then displays this output:

```
PS    C:\>    C:\Scripts\ListStoppedServices.ps1    N*The
following N* services are stopped on PLANX:Name
DisplayName----          -----------NetDDE          Network
DDENetDDEdsdm          Network DDE DSDMNtLmSsp
NT LM Security Support ProviderNtmsSvc          Removable
StoragePS C:\>
```

This script is a bit more complex because it can filter the
stopped services based on the given string to clean the
output. This script is not a complex automation component,
but it only shows some of the power PowerShell has. To
use this power, you need to understand the functionality of
PowerShell better so that you can write more complex and
meaningful scripts.

Making scripts useful, phase 1: Variables

Therefore, if you purchase that the whole point of scripting is to do things consistently again and again, then you have to buy the idea that you want to do different things the same thing. But how do you change the things you're doing? How are the variables? Variables are kinds of holders, and you can put in the values, words, numbers, essentially anything.

Variables in PowerShell always have a dollar sign) ($in front of them.

Let me declare— in other words, first set up— a couple of variables right now for you:

$name = 'Jon'

Volume 0%

$number = 12345

$location = 'Charlotte'

$listofnumbers = 6,7,8,9

$my_last_math_grade = 'D+'

To declare these variables, all I have to do is add a dollar sign, then use whatever name I like for the variable. In essence, no spaces in that name are allowed-and then space, a sign equal, a different space, then whatever I want the value of the variable. If I want a variable with the meaning of the text, I must add one quote from each side of the text. (There are a few variations, but my aim here is to keep it simple, so we're going to stick to it for the time being.) You can only declare a variable without any value. This form of name reserves the word, which is probably more useful when you are in the middle of creation than any other time. Do you know what other attributes you can bring in? The performance of cmdlet, which is a nice moniker which refers to the simplest bit of. Net-based code you can execute, which returns either the PowerShell prompt or a script. The Get-Process cmdlet list all processes, for example, while the Get-PSSnapin cmdlet displays the new functionality of all existing PowerShell snap-ins.

To find out how many cmdlets the machine has, we can use:

```
(get-command).count
```
And at least for the program, I've written today, and the result has been 1,338 cmdlets.

Let's declare a store variable that counts in. We're going to call it.

$numberofcmdlets

And let's store the output (get-command). Count entry in that variable.

$numberofcmdlets = (get-command).count

If you enter its name in the prompt, PowerShell will tell you the current value of any variable. So let's see if it worked.

Access! Access! You can now use this variable as part of another. Let's look for a simple example at the Write-Host cmdlet, which writes text to the PowerShell session screen on the desktop. Write-Host has a lot of skills, but you can only tell in its simplest way:

Write-Host "Whatever text I want, as long as it is inside double quotes."

You can cut and paste this line into a PowerShell window, and it will come out exactly as it does.

But you can combine Write-Host variables. You call them with the dollar sign and work them in your text. I can tell, for example:

Write-Host "There are $numberofcmdlets commands available for use on this system."

Let us now set aside variables and proceed to the next scripting element: decision-making and looping.

Making scripts useful, phase 2: If/Then, Do-While and ForEach

In reality, the next step lets you do some magic. We now know how to store values in variables, but we have to do other things for those variables. Let's take a look. Let's take a look.

If / then The easiest decision-making process in PowerShell is the if / then mechanism; in PowerShell lingo, it's called "construction."

You format it by parenthesizing it, putting a curly left bracelet on a new line alone, adding the PowerShell cmdlets or actions to perform if this act's right, starting in a new line, and ending with a curly right brace on a new line. The key points here are: The comparison argument will contain either TRUE or FALSE logical answers. Speak of it as a matter of yes or no. If you have to do something not based on a question of yes or no, it is necessary to build another loop; we are going to cover that in a bit.

The code that works if your statement is YES or NO must be in curly braces, and it is best to put these curly braces on their own to match them if you type more complicated scripts.

For instance, if I wanted to compare two numbers— let's say 5 and 10— if PowerShell was to show whether ten were larger than 5, then we could write the following if / then build:

```
If (10 –gt 5)
{
Write-Host "Yes"
}
```

You might already know –gt is the "greater than" PowerShell switch. We also used Write-Host in the previous example.

It's easy and probably won't be a big help to you in your administrative tasks. You may add more "nests" to the If / Then block to make the construction somewhat more usable. Once, they execute gradually— this is known as a sequential construct in programming so that one comparison must be made, then the next, and when you finish the similarities end.

It looks like this:

```
If (10 –gt 11)
{
Write-Host "Yes"
} elseif (11 –gt 10)
{
Write-Host "This time, yes"
}
```

You should be able to follow that one pretty easily; here is the result.

The first logical comparison (is ten greater than 11? No) is false, so PowerShell moves on to the next one via the elseif comparison, which is PowerShell parlance for "next, please!" (is 11 greater than 10? Yes), and prints the Write-Host line I wrote for that test.

In constructs like these, when you're testing, it's best to have a different output for each test. If I had chosen Yes for both constructs, and then run the script, I would not have been able to tell which comparison test was producing the

Yes -- there's no differentiation. Here, I added, "This time," so I could tell what was happening in the script.

You can include a bunch of these else if blocks in your script -- theoretically, there is no maximum. It's a great way to establish conditions before you do something. For instance, if I wanted to move mailboxes only where the user's region was in the United States, then I could use an IF statement to get at the mailbox properties and then write the code for the move within the curly braces.

Or maybe I have a machine with a pesky startup problem because of an interaction with an old piece of software. So I need to write a script that I set off as a scheduled task that checks a service after a minute or two and, if it is stopped (there's my comparison), starts the service (there's my code).

Hopefully, you can see the applications of this type of PowerShell construct.

Finally, you can choose to include an else block in your if/then construct, which runs as basically the alternative ending for your script -- if all of the ifs and elseifs do not evaluate and run their code, then the else block can do something to conclude the script. The else block is written at the very end and DOES NOT include a parenthetical comparison statement; you leave it off.

Here's an example: I might make a series of comparisons like this, and then make a statement of exasperation at the end:

```
If (10 –gt 11)
{
Write-Host "Yes"
} elseif (11 –lt 10)
{
Write-Host "This time, yes"
} elseif (20 –gt 40)
{
Write-Host "Third time was a charm"
} else {
Write-Host "You're really terrible at math, aren't you?"
}
```

Do while

Do, While is the simplest of PowerShell looping constructs. A looping construct is essentially a piece of code that works on several different subjects over and over— in other words, and it loops over several things, does something for each, until some situation changes or that set of things is exhausted.

In PowerShell, there are two main types of loops—— a Do While Loop and the other I will explain.

Do While it's just a construct that says to PowerShell, "do this until some state I'm telling you that this is real." It's so easy.

There are two ways to build this house. You can put Do, and a curly left brace on one line, starting from a new line after the curly left-brace if you want to execute at least once commands and then as often as required to fulfill any requirement you set. And then, put the right curly strap on a new line, followed by your conditional statement in parenthesis. Also, the conditional declaration must be true or false.

Let's set a variable called numbers, for example, and give it the first value.

$numbers = 1

Let us then configure a simple Do While building that adds 1 to any number in that variable already, until the variable is number 10.

Do {$numbers = $numbers + 1Write-Host "The current value of the variable is $numbers"
} While ($numbers –lt 10)

You can also set up a Do While construct so that your order set only works when the condition is valid. You have to delete the do sentence and use it only while.

While ($numbers –lt 10) {$numbers = $numbers + 1
Write-Host "The current value of the variable is $numbers"}

Foreach
ForEach is the other structure of looping. ForEach looks at a set of things one at a time, and then if you say so, perform some action or collection of commands on it.
This is how to think about it. Let's assume that you had a list of users from your HR department who had quit in the last quarter. You need to deactivate your account in Active

147

Directory. To do this, you can use a ForEach loop. You would like to say: Dear PowerShell, my ForEach User List (in this list)

{disable their log on ability in Active Directory}

Notice the familiar curly braces and their location. (Developer talk shows you how to write code without taking the time to figure out the proper syntax, as well as how to make sure you have a good game plan when dealing with a problem you will ultimately need to write code for solving.) A different part of the ForEach loop is the keyword. This tells PowerShell to create a single variable that holds the values for your bigger set one by one.

Let's look at an example of real code. Let's use a basic variable name package.

When we make a list in a variable, we created what is referred to as an array, which is just one big type of matrix that has been stored in the memory of PowerShell, which enables it to store a lot of things at one time.

Let us also start a count variable, so that we get a sense of how the loop goes.

Let's then use the ForEach loop to count the number of names we have. $count=0 Remember our keyword— we have to create a new variable to name whatever we want. It contains every single name which comes from the list of names we saved in the $names variable. I also referred to this new variable $singlename to indicate that it is a new variable that contains only one value from a set. PowerShell deals with that single value, then continue, catches another value from the larger list, transfers it to the new single variable, acts on it on any commands you have placed in the loop, and then laters, rinses and repeats.

ForEach ($singlename in $names) {
$count += 1Write-Host "$singlename"}
The+= shorthand essentially means that in this case, I increase the number by any interval I put next. I have then inserted a Write-Host line with the $singlename variable to see the value of the PowerShell loop.
Finally, after the end (after the curly right brace, that is), I'm going to add a simple writing-host thread, so we'll be able to answer our question.

Write-Host "The total number of names is $count."

Concepts For Powershell Scripting

PowerShell scripts provide a convenient way to automate different tasks. Here are some key concepts to help beginners build PowerShell scripts.

PS1 files

A PowerShell script is just a simple text file. The file contains a set of PowerShell commands that appear on a separate line with each command. The text file must use the. PS1 extension to handle the text file as a PowerShell script.

Execution permissions

PowerShell enforces an execution policy to prevent the execution of malicious scripts. The execution policy is described by default as limited so that PowerShell scripts are not running. The current execution policy can be calculated by using the following cmdlet: Get-ExecutionPolicy.

Restricted-Scripts are not going to run.

RemoteSigned-The locally generated scripts are not working, but they are not downloaded from the Internet (except if they are signed digitally by a trusted publisher).

AllSigned-Scripts are only executed when a trusted author has signed them.

Unrestricted-Scripts run independently of where they came from and whether they are signed.

You can set the execution policy of PowerShell by using the following cmdlet:

Set-ExecutionPolicy <policy name>

Running a script

If you tried to execute an executable file from the command line for years, you had to go to the directory of the file and then enter the executable file name. This ancient method does not work for PowerShell scripts, however.

If you want to execute a PowerShell script, the complete path with the filename is usually entered. You can type C:\Scrips\Script.ps1, for example, to run a script called SCRIPT.PS1, if the folder containing the script is in the path of your code, you can execute it by typing its name. You can also use a shortcut if you are already in the script tab. You should enter.\ and the name of the script instead of entering the whole path of the script in such a case. You may, for example, type:.\Script.ps1

Pipelining

The pipeline is the term for feeding the output of one command into another. It allows the second command to function on the received information. Clearly distinguish two commands (or cmdlets) with a pipe symbol).

To order to understand how pipelining works, imagine constructing a list of processes on a server and sorting the list by process identifier. Use the Get-Process cmdlet to obtain a list of methods, but the list will not be classified. Nonetheless, the list will be sorted if you pipeline the output of the cmdlet into the Sort-Object ID command. This is how the list of commands used looks:

Get-Process | Sort-Object ID

Variables

Although pipelining may be used to feed the output of one command into another, pipelining alone sometimes won't do the job. When a command is piped into another command, the output is used immediately. Sometimes you may need to save the production for a while so you can use it (or reuse) later. Variables come into play here. It is easy to see a variable as a repository to store a value, but a variable in PowerShell can store the full output of a command. For example, assume that you want to save the list of processes running as a variable on a server. This line of code can be used for this: $a= Get-Process The variable here is called $a. If the variable is to be used, call it by name. For instance, typing $a prints the contents of the variable on the screen. You may add a variable to the final output of several pipeline commands. Encircle the instructions with parentheses. For example, you could use the command $a= (Get-Process Sort-Object ID) to sort running processes by Process ID and then assign the result to a variable

The @ symbol
You may transform the contents of a list into an array with the @ symbol. For example, take the following code line to make a variable named $Procs containing several text lines (an array): $procs= @{name=" explorer," svchost"} Also, you can take the @ symbol to make sure that the variable is viewed as an array instead of as a single value. For example, the code line below runs the cmdlet of the Get-

Process against the variable I specified just now. This way, all Windows processes used by Windows Explorer and Svchost are shown. Note how the @ symbol is used before the variable name instead of the dollar sign we usually see used:

Get-Process @procs

Split

The split operator divides a text string based on the specified character. Suppose, for example, and you want to split a phrase into a table consisting of every single word in the phrase. You can do this with a command like this:

"This is a test" -split " "

The result would look like this:

This

is

a

test

Join

Just as divided text strings can be divided into different components, the joining operator may combine multiple text blocks into one. This section, for example, generates a text string with my first and last name:

"Brien","Posey" -join " "

At the end of the instruction, the space between the quotes tells Windows to insert a space between the two text strings.

Breakpoints

If the script contains bugs, running a newly created PowerShell script might have unintended consequences. One way to protect yourself is to introduce breakpoints in your script at strategic locations. Thus, you should ensure that the script works as intended before the whole thing is processed. The line number is the easiest way to insert a breakpoint. For example, to insert a breakpoint on the 10th line of a file, you could use a command like this: New-PSBreakpoint-Script C:\Scripts\Script.ps1-Line 10. So you could use a command like this, New-PSBreakpoint-Script C:\script\Script.ps1, to break every time the contents of a$ were modified. A Note I wasn't including a dollar sign after the variable name.

There's a variety of PSBreakpoint verbs that you can use, such as Create, Get, Activate, Disable and Remove.

Step

It may often be appropriate to execute the script line by line when debugging a script. To do this, you can use the cmdlet step-in. This causes the script to pause after each paragraph, whether or not there is a breakpoint. You can use Step-Out cmdlet to avoid Windows from accessing the script when you're finished. Nonetheless, breakpoints are still handled even after using the Step-Out cmdlet.

However, if your script uses functions, the step-over cmdlet may be of interest to you. Step-Over functions like step-in, but Windows won't go through it if a feature is called. The whole system runs smoothly.

Choosing a Scripting Language

Several scripting languages can be used to automate processes. Depending on your process automation needs, one language is preferred over other languages, or several languages will suit well. To start evaluating the language you want to use, you should begin by understanding the type of systems your process is using. For example, if tasks are performed on Microsoft Windows-based systems, you may see that the proprietary scripting language of Microsoft, PowerShell, suits your needs perfectly. The.

NET platform is used by PowerShell and offers great power and flexibility for process automation.

While you work in a predominantly UNIX-based environment, a UNIX-based scripting language like shell scripts can make sense. These scripting languages are usually specific to a particular shell interpreter and are often not easily transferred between various UNIX shells. Furthermore, shell scripts can not migrate to Microsoft Windows systems just as Microsoft PowerShell can't adapt to UNIX-based systems.

It highlights one of the biggest problems with the use of system-specific scripting languages. The scripts are typically not portable between various operating systems. This may not be a concern if your process automation focuses on one operating system, but more prominent companies struggle with heterogeneous environments of multiple operating systems. If this is so, selecting a scripting language that runs on several operating systems platforms will make more sense.

There are a variety of languages available in this field, but some of the most common are Perl, PowerShell, Ruby, and PHP among company application managers. There is constant discussion of which language is best used for which function, but most of them are process automation tasks. If you want to use a cross-platform scripting language, such as one, the language option is to decide which this can carry out the functions that you want to execute easily, which is used for other previously performed process automation and the functions you know best. Some scripting languages have functions or modules which make it easier to perform specific tasks. The availability of these functions or modules will affect your choice of language. For starters, the Perl language uses modules available through the Comprehensive Perl Archive Network (CPAN). You can manually write code for this in your process automation if you need to collect information from a Cisco product and decode the version information, or you can use the Cisco:: Version Module from CPAN to do the work for you. An example of code demonstrating this is:

```
use strict;
use Cisco::Version;
## Load the output of the "show version" command into a
string
my $show_version = $inbound_data;
## Create a new Cisco::Version object
```

```
my $sv = Cisco::Version->new($show_version);
## Parse the output
$sv->parse();
## Print the amount of RAM found
print "total DRAM memory = ", $sv->get_memory(), "\n";
```

Every scripting language has its modular libraries, integrated features, a variety of tutorials, and a support group. If you use a language selection method based on available modules or functions, you will decide what the script is for and then evaluate what resources are available to do that. There can be a scripting language that suits very well on what you find.

If you or someone else in your company used a particular scripting language to automate the process, it might make sense to use the same language. You develop the versatility and capacity to use a variety of languages in an organization, but you begin to break your organizational experience. Remember your role as a business application administrator and how simple it is to support a variety of applications compared with specializing in a single application. The same goes for the selection of a scripting language. If the team already knows how to use one language, you can use that language even if it's not necessarily the best way to make it easier for the future. Nonetheless, if there is a driving reason why an existing language doesn't work, a new scripting language may be worth adding for the team.

Finally, your understanding of a language plays a role in the language selection process. It might make sense to stick to the information and automate your processes using PowerShell if you are very good at coding in PowerShell. On the other hand, learning new languages is often beneficial to extend your knowledge. This often comes down to how eager you are to learn something new and how long it takes to learn the new script language.

Powershell Is Not AScripting Language

Even if you're not a hands-on IT professional any longer, you certainly know that. The text-based GUI on the command line was around even before the first GUI appeared. Indeed, today's Windows PowerShell-enabled nth-generation command line now has many near-graphical elements of its own.

PowerShell is incredibly strong for Windows. A qualified professional can quickly create a useful one-line command with today's Windows PowerShell. This individual line will contact remote machines, communicate with the Active Directory, perform one or more activities, and report back with an entity completely controlled and ultimately take the form of a dynamically-built table, a list of data, or even an exported. CSV or. An XML document that can be used in certain external IT applications. Using the pipeline magic, the same Windows PowerShell specialist will combine a series of cmdlets to fuel up elegantly the output from one cmdlet–all the way down the pipeline to a conclusion.

But, with all its beauty and strength, why aren't there more Windows PowerShell IT professionals today? When it is feasible–and indeed possible–to do so much with so little, why are more IT professionals not lining up in a lot to learn and take advantage of their ridiculously powerful abilities? I believe Windows PowerShell has a problem with perception.

I have only recently discovered this issue of perception. In recent months, another Redmond writer, Don Jones, and I have been hired to develop a training program for Windows PowerShell by a major software provider. Thanks to almost complete versatility in developing the courseware, Jones and I have taken a step back from both the Microsoft message and the online content of many of their aficionados. We had to decide the essence of Windows PowerShell to explain its capabilities to students better.

Absolute precision

Once we looked at the scripts, ideas for scripting, and constructs you're able to find on the Internet today practically all over the world, Jones and I realized that the problem is that it's a scripting language for the uninitiated. But it isn't. This confusion is not healthy. Consider how IT neophytes interpret scripting languages for a minute. Solutions such as batch, KiXtart, and VBScript are all considered to be the most popular scripting languages in Windows history. While strong, these languages are too complex, too difficult to learn, and a potential source of disasters if not completely treated, for today's newly acclaimed IT professionals. They don't have their feelings far from reality. We all heard the stories of languages like VBScript about how some wrong characters triggered huge deletion–or the whole server reboot script, which was launched somehow in the middle of the day. VBScript and others did not have their security problems with automatic deployment and listening in insecure runtime environments on each Windows desktop and server.

As a result, entire industries have built management software to simplify the IT professionals ' jobs without the nasty scripting GUI. For many, the whole scripting mechanism has been demonized to the point where it was even deactivated.

Administrative automation

So what is it if Windows PowerShell isn't a scripting language?

I claim that Windows PowerShell 2.0 is an administrative text-based automation solution. Even the greenest of IT professionals can speed up the completion of the most daunting IT tasks by simply adding a few main cmdlets.

Take the common problem of adding new AD users and providing them with access to one or more global organizations, for example. To accomplish that task today with the Windows GUI, every user-generated needs a collection of mouse clicks. Information needs to be entered many times, increasing the likelihood of error.

The time required to complete the task often rises in line with the number of users to build. This process takes so much time that many of the above graphically focused management solutions have created their wizards to build batch users.

Taking the beauty of this simple Windows PowerShell command into consideration:

Import-CSV newusers.csv | New-

ADUser -passthru | Enable-ADAc

count -passthru | Add-ADGroup

Member "New Users"

This command reads the list of new users included in an Excel spreadsheet. CSV file in a single line. It pipes the users to the New-ADUser cmdlet, then pipes them again to Enable-ADAccount and then completes the loop by filling in the entire Add-ADGroupMember result for adding their account to the global new user's group. Four commands on a single line have accomplished the mission using the same table of users that you've received from your HR department. I must admit that the title of this column is not entirely true. Indeed, Windows PowerShell is packed with powerful scripting designs to perform all your tasks in a scripting language. Yet Windows PowerShell is something much superior to a scripting language at its very core. It's a not-so-difficult method for easily completing regular IT activities without repetitive steps and error risk.

Therefore, if you haven't looked at Windows PowerShell yet for fear of a new language, give it another chance. You may find it easier and more satisfying than you expect.

POWERSHELL FOR USERS: BASIC SYNTAX — CMDLETS

This chapter is intended for developers who want to provide a control-line management framework for system administrators. Windows PowerShell provides a simple way to build management commands that expose objects to the. NET framework and allows Windows PowerShell to do most of the work. Many people believe that PowerShell is essentially CMD-prompt 2.0 because of its look, but it is really a fully working scripting language below.

For people with programming experience, learning PowerShell can be very useful. Whether you're a developer, a dev-ops or an admin, you can make serious use of understanding PowerShell. You may think that this is just an eyecatcher-colored version of the command prompt, but it is really a full scripting language with lots of good tie ins.

PowerShell has what is called a cmdlet, which is basically the same concept as functions from other languages.

I would presume that you come from a more formal language and are used to naming these functions:

MyFunction(Value, Value, Value)

If you used cmdlets like this in PowerShell, you did it wrong. This could lead you to experience some serious problems.

"But I can type Get-Service("alg") and it works just fine!"

Perhaps, but PowerShell is just doing a few fun parsing tricks. This does not work with every cmdlet or set of (overload) parameters of those cmdlets.

There's a lot of helpful little tricks and shortcuts that I can use to shorten lines as well, and as we go, I'll point to some of the common ones.

Here are some basics of cmdlets you should learn about:

POWERSHELL IS NOT CASE SENSITIVE: Get-command, get-command, and GeT-CoMmaNd are the same cmdlets that are always in the verb-noun form to help you understand what you're doing without having to look at the aid of your data PowerShell call its parameters "parameter." This means they often start command-

independent names with a dash like —name, —computer name, —force.
#these will work the same, despite the order difference
get-service -name "ALG" -ComputerName "localhost"
get-service -ComputerName "localhost" -name "ALG"

Certain parameters have no meaning and are called switch parameters (such as as-force, -verbose, etc.) these are the default settings and are only called-Force parameters.

#this will fail if notepad isn't open
stop-process -name notepad —whatif

Many parameters are set to "positional," allowing us to avoid writing the name of the parameter (-ComputerName, -Name,-Whatever) and to provide only the values. In this case, the order varies, so instead, you can still call them directly. I'll teach you how to classify them later, but if you see that people do, you know it's a shortcut.

#these are the same
get-service -name "alg"
get-service "ALG"

Another common shortcut is, PowerShell can sometimes assume, even if you forget about quotes, that something you type is a string. A good rule of thumb is that you can consider a string data parameter that would allow you to skip the quotation (as long as you have no spaces or odd special characters). When PowerShell screams at you, just quotes, but it explains why you usually see such things as these:

#no quotes + positional parameter = short line
get-service alg

You can use the TechNet documentation to display the syntax for a cmdlet or look at the shell using another cmdlet:
get-command -name "get-service" –Syntax

If you execute this command yourself, several syntax blocks with different parameters will come back. These are sets of parameters that you can see as overloads.
We can use the support cmdlet to see more detailed information + examples + definitions of parameters. Use

the-ShowWindow switch parameter to make your life easier.

Get-help Get-Service –showWindow

If you followed them, then all you need to know about cmdlets is that.

Recognize that the long-service is the way to write the most readability stuff. Still, the shortcuts are common and valuable if you do things like MyFunction (value, value), you should stop and get on the correct syntax car to save yourself issues.

There are a couple of other notes worth mentioning regarding cmdlets and basic PowerShell syntax:

PowerShell contains Aliases that are alternate names for cmdlets. Many of these exist to make language adoption simpler. These will be anchored back to other shell commands (CMD, terminal, etc.) or different language programming paradigms. Here are a few common ones that you probably used or saw:

Things such as you are popular for CMD, but Get-Childitem is unintuitive and removes the alias.

Aliases will take the parameters the same way as their CMDLETs: consider using full cmdlet names in your scripts as a good practice, since not everyone knows aliases. Nonetheless, it might be easier to understand for some, such as Dir, CD, etc. than the actual cmdlet. Take advantage of your best judgment.

If you ever see something, not like VERB-NOUN, it's probably an alias that you can watch with get-command and get-alias.

#all do the same thing
Get-ChildItem -Path c:\
dir -Path c:\
ls -Path c:\
gci -Path c:\
get-command dir

CommandType Name Version Source

----------- ---- ------- ------

Alias dir -> Get-ChildItem

External commands, such as icacls, ipconfig, etc. all live on the PowerShell path. It spins a new process when it's called, but if necessary, you can use it in your script. Don't try because the syntax is far less consistent than real cmdlets.

Scripting Languages Vs Programming Languages: Powershell

The compiler-using programming languages and the Interpreter-using script languages.

The compiler and the interpreter concentrate on what exactly they are and what role they play.

The high-level language is translated to machine language by a compiler, which is the interpreter? The obvious question is, therefore, whether there is a disparity between programming languages and scripting languages? Yeah, but they operate in a different way than the compiler and interpreter.

This HLL is not approved by the program so that we can translate these HLL into machine languages by the compiler. Such computer languages have a fake binary name. What is in 0's and 1's form?

By compiling HLL to machine language, the interpreter does almost the same thing, but it does so line-by-line.

Until we discuss the difference between programming and scripting languages, it is obvious why these languages were born, what were the developers ' needs?

Programming languages for Microsoft Excel, Microsoft Word, PowerPoint, Internet browsers, etc. (took these words for easy understanding) were initially written. Thus the program codes were designed using different languages such as Java, C, C++, etc. Such software codes were important for users to add new functionality, there must be an alternative to provide the appropriate interface to their bye code, and so it led to the start of the scripting languages. Scripting languages are a sort of programming language not needed— an explicit compilation phase. The example below provides a useful insight into the reader's comprehension.

In the normal case, for instance, if you have a C++ program, you must first compile it before you can run it. Similarly, you do not need to compile it before you run if you have a JavaScript program. This makes it clear that JavaScript is a scripting language.

Head to head comparison between programming languages vs scripting languages

There are 5 PL (programming languages)[Types] subcategories for First / Second / Third / Fourth / Fifth generation PL. In contrast, SC[Scripting languages] has scripting languages both on the server-side and on the client-side.

The PL supports.

Explicit data type support,

Rich user interface support,

Explicit, graphic design support,

SL implicit data types support,

Limited user interface design support,

No graphic design support.

From applicability

It is more consistent with mathematical formulas while implementing code while SL automates a specific task within a system and extracts data from a data set.

The SL is a subset of PL that can be said after all the above-listed points have been tested. The execution environment is the deciding factor in determining a disparity between programming and scripting languages. Scripts are usually written to control the behavior of the application, and the programming languages are used to construct an application.

MODULES

One of the basic principles in PowerShell that simplifies the development and versatility of programs is the principle of modularity, according to which the program is divided into separate named blocks, called modules. The modules allow you to divide complex tasks into smaller ones. They are designed to provide users with reusable functionalities (interfaces) in the form of a set of routines, variables, classes, and more. A program that has a modular structure usually consists of a set of modules, among which are the main module.

Consequently, modules perform at least two important functions:

✓ Reuse the code without explicitly duplicating it.

✓ Address space management - a module is a high-level organization of programs that avoids conflicts in naming variables, functions, classes, etc.

In PowerShell, a module is a separate file containing the source code - variables, routines, classes, algorithms and more. Therefore, creating your own module is no different than writing a regular program in a separate file. All module objects can be used in the main program or other modules. You need to import them to do this. You can import the module completely or its individual objects. Import is done using the module name. The module name is the file name without the extension ".py".

IMPORT AND USE OF MODULES

Import Module

By this time, we have repeatedly used functions from different modules and already know that the module is imported using the import keyword: here the module is the name of the module. Generally, the module import instruction is placed at the beginning of the program.

import modul

During such import, we get access to all elements of the imported module. Each module creates its own namespace, which is a global scope for all objects defined in it.

Importing a module actually starts executing the program contained in the module. Therefore, it is not recommended to import modules obtained from untrusted sources. Doing so may damage the data on your computer.

In order to prevent the objects of this module from being in conflict with other global names or other modules, when accessing module elements, you must use a prefix consisting of a module name with a period, for example

here the module is the name of the module, func1 is the function contained in this module.

modul.func1()

One import instruction can import multiple modules. In this case, the module names are listed by comma:

import math print(math.pi)

However, this approach is not recommended as it reduces the readability of the code. Compare the visual import instructions above with the one above

import modul_1

import modul_2

import modul_3

Using Aliases

If the module name is too long or might conflict with other program objects, you can create an alias for it using the as keyword:

import math as m

In this case, all elements of this module become available in the program through the name m, not through math:

print(m.pi) # the math prefix is m

In fact, creating a module alias is changing the module name when imported.

Importing Individual Module Items

PowerShell has the ability to connect not only the module, but its individual elements. To do this, use the from instruction, which has the following syntax

from modul import obj

here the module is the name of the module, obj is the object (variable, function, class, etc.) contained in this module.

from math import pi

print(pi)   # The math prefix is not specified

When imported using the from instruction, the object is accessible by name obj (no prefix, as opposed to importing the entire module). Example

from math import pi, e, factorial

You can import multiple objects from one module at a time. The imported objects are then comma-separated

 from math import *

```
print(pi)        # the math prefix is not specified
print(factorial(4)) # the math prefix is not specified
```

The instructions for importing all the objects of the module are used. The difference with standard module imports is that all module objects are accessible by their prefixed names (without the module name).

```
from math import factorial as f
print(f(4))
```

When importing individual items, using the from instruction, you can create aliases for them using the as keyword. Example, Also, using aliases solves the problem of importing objects from different modules that have the same name. Importing module objects using the from instruction makes the imported objects read-only.

Re-Import Modules

It should be remembered that the module loads only once during program execution, no matter how many times the instruction to import it occurs in the program. The download occurs when the first import instruction is executed and all subsequent import operations of this module will return the already loaded module object, even if the module itself has been modified.

Therefore, if you need to re-import the module, use the importlib module's reload () instruction:

from importlib import reload

reload(modul)

CREATING MODULES

As it became clear, creating your own module does not require any additional effort from the programmer. However, there are a few rules to keep in mind when creating your own modules:

When naming a module, you must follow the same rules as when creating variables - only Latin letters, numbers and " _ " can be used, with the first character in the module name not being a number.

The module cannot be named because it has built-in functions or keywords.

The module must be located on the file system so that it can be accessed for import from your application or other modules that use it.

Consider an example of creating a module that describes two functions - raising a number to a square and a cube. Let's create a PowerShell code file named my_module.py:

def my_pow2(x):

```
return x ** 2


def my_pow3(x):

return x ** 3
```

My_module is ready. We will use it in our program. Let's create another file named main.py that will contain the following code

```
import my_module    # import module


res2 = my_module.my_pow2(2.0)  # using the function from the module
 res3 = my_module.my_pow3(2.0)  # using the function from the module
```

THE MAIN MODULE OF THE PROGRAM

The main one is the module from which the program starts. Unlike imported ones, whose name is the same as the file it contains, the main module has a reserved name "main". This name is contained in a special variable name that is created during import or run for each module.

As noted earlier, when you import a module, its code is fully executed. Therefore, module name analysis allows or not to execute specific sets of instructions, depending on whether the module is the master. For example, if the interpreter executes such code

```
if name       == " main ":
   process_some_code
```

the process_some_code instruction set will only be executed if the program executes as the main module and not the imported one.

Placement Of Modules In The File System.

PowerShell is distributed with a standard module library of more than one 200 modules. They provide support for tasks such as operating system interface, object management, networking, Internet, graphical interface, and more.

Standard modules are built into the interpreter. All you need to do is import them into the program with the import command.

In addition to the standard ones, there are a number of custom modules that are designed to handle a variety of tasks. Such modules need to be further installed. The procedure for installing such a module depends

from the operating system used and usually described in the module documentation.

When importing a module, the interpreter searches for the module file in folders in the following order

Among standard plug-ins (PowerShell directories).

In the folder of the program importing the module.

In the folders specified in the POWERSHELLPATH operating system environment variable.

The list of these folders is contained in the sys.path variable.

So, while running your application, you can expand the directory list where the interpreter will look for modules to import by adding a new directory to sys.path.

```
>>> import sys
>>> print(sys.path)
['D:\\Repository\\Test',
'C:\\IDE\\PowerShell\\PowerShell35.zip',
'C:\\IDE\\PowerShell\\DLLs',    'C:\\IDE\\PowerShell\\lib',
'C:\\IDE\\PowerShell',          'C:\\IDE\\PowerShell\\lib\\site-
packages']
```

You can also specify or supplement the POWERSHELLPATH environment variable in the operating system by navigating to directories where custom modules are located.

```
>>> sys.path.append('C:/my_modules')
```

PACKAGES

A package is a way of structuring the namespace of modules based on the file system. So, if modules are files containing source code, then packages are directories containing modules. Bundles are formed in the form of a hierarchy of folders containing the module.

Packages allow you to structure collections of modules that form large libraries - batch importing makes the code more readable and significantly speeds up the search. The application of packages makes it safe to use module names in multimodal packages.

In order to import a module, you must specify the full path (including all package directories) to the module being imported through the "." (dot). For example, importing lib.py from Client will look like this:

>>> import TCP.Client.lib

The reference to the function in the program must also be complete:

>>> TCP.Client.lib.connect()

This method is often not convenient because of its cumbersome nature, so it is recommended that you use the alias (alias) mechanism described above when importing. Example,

>>> import TCP.Client.lib as cl_lib

Then calling the connect () function from the imported module will look like this

 >>> cl_lib.connect()

Also note that the package contains two modules with the same name - lib.py. However, due to the method of importing modules, no conflicts in the program will occur - the two modules are in different folders of the package.

TASKS FOR INDEPENDENT WORK

$\ln 4 + e3 - \sin 33 / 2 \cos 2 + ch4$.

Describe the module for working with square matrices and vectors. In the module, describe the following:

I / O operations:

a) reading the vector from the keyboard;

b) reading the matrix from the keyboard;

c) reading a vector from a text file;

d) reading the matrix from a text file;

e) displaying the vector on the screen;

f) display the matrix;

g) writing the vector to a text file;

h) writing the matrix into a text file; operations with vectors and matrices:

a) matrix multiplication;

b) multiplying the matrix by the vector;

c) multiplying the vector by a number;

d) multiplication of the vector by the matrix;

e) multiplying the i-th row of the matrix by the number a;

f) rearranging the i-th and j-th rows of the matrix;

g) rearranging the i-th and j-th columns of the matrix;

h) adding to the i-th row of the matrix the j-th row multiplied by the number a;

i) obtaining the row of the matrix;

j) subtracting the vector from all rows of the matrix. Using the Solution module:

a) Convert the matrix into upper triangular linear transformations;

b) Determine the rank of the matrix;

c) Calculate the determinant of the matrix;

d) Calculate the inverted matrix.

Describe the module for working with points and segments on the plane. Point and segment types are represented as tuples:

Point - (x, y) Line - (a, b)

where a, b are points. Take action on points:

a) take the point t;

b) put the point t equal to (x, y);

c) show the point t. Take action on segments:

a) take the segment s;

b) show segment s;

c) put the segment s equal to a, b;

d) length of segment s;

e) whether the point t lies on one line with segment s;

f) is the point t inside the segment s;

g) the area of the triangle formed by the point t and the segment s.

The file records the sequence of points. Using the point and line segment module, find:

a) the triangle with the largest area formed by the points of the sequence;

b) the circle of the smallest radius within which all points of the sequence lie;

c) the segment with the largest number of consecutive points;

d) the circle on which the largest number of consecutive points lie.

Implement a module for working with polynomials Pn (x) of degree n. Implement polynomial as a list of coefficients. The module performs the following operations:

a) read the polynomial Pn (x);

b) show polynomialPn (x);

c) determine the polynomial мa (x) for the given зада;

d) find the derivative $P'(x)$ of the polynomial $P(x)$;

n n

e) find the original Fn (x) polynomial Pn (x) satisfying the condition Fn $(0) = c,$

where c is a given real number;

f) find the sum of two polynomials;

g) find the product of two polynomials;

h) carry out the division operation with the remainder of the two polynomials. Using the described module, solve the problems:

a) the distance traveled by a material point in time t is determined by the law s $(t) = Pn$ (t); determine its speed at time момент;

b) the velocity of the point at time t is determined by the law v $(t) =$

Pn (t); determine what distance the point will pass for the time interval $[t1, t2]$;

c) find the derivative of order k from the polynomial Pn (x);

d) determine the largest common divisor of two polynomials Pn (x) and Rn (x);

e) determine the least common multiple of two polynomials;

f) solve the Cauchy problem for the ordinary differential equation

y (k) = Pn (x), $x \geq x0$, y $(x0)$ = $y0$,. . . , y $(k-1)$ $(x0)$ = $yk-1$.

WHAT IS POWERSHELL ISE

The Windows PowerShell Integrated Scripting Environment (ISE) is a Windows PowerShell host program. In the ISE, you can execute commands and write, check and debug scripts in one graphical user interface based on Windows. The ISE offers multi-line editing, tab completion, syntax coloring, selective implementation, context-sensitive assistance, and right-to-left language support. Menu items and keyboard shortcuts are mapped to the same functions in the Windows PowerShell console. You can, for instance, right-click on a line of code in the editing pane to create a breakpoint while debugging a script in ISE. The Windows PowerShell Integrated Scripting Framework is a graphical user interface and front-ends Windows PowerShell hosting program. The ISE enables developers to run PowerShell commands to build, check, and refine PowerShell scripts with no need to work directly within the conventional PowerShell command-line interface (CLI). The ISE offers various editing tools, user assistance, and other user-friendly features not easily available in PowerShell. The ISE supports, for instance, multi-line editing, tab completion, coloring based on syntax, selective running, context-sensible assistance, and multi-language support. Windows PowerShell ISE is an environment for scripting and writing, screening, and checking in a single Windows graphical user interface that includes multi-line editing, tab completing, syntax coloring, selective execution, context-sensitive help, and support. The ISE Menu Options and keyboard shortcuts are identical to many of the common tasks performed in a PowerShell console.

Powershell ISE Features

Below is a standard Windows 10 PowerShell ISE. The traditional console area— the Panel of the Console— is delineated into dark blue. Still, a selection of common file and display controls is located along the top toolbar, including buttons to activate the remote PowerShell sound as well as a conventional PowerShell console for the ISE. Developers may find an alphabetical command by filterable command group, to type all appropriate parameters in the right panel. The command is filterable. The correctly configured command can then be inserted into the console without having to type the full command manually.

A second key function of ISE 2.0 is to support up to 32 running environments. Only up to eight previous ISE versions were supported. This may seem like a great deal of multi-tasking, but developers can use this ability to work with similar scripts and make real-time adjustments. At the same time, they see the immediate effects of their modifications across other related scripts. For example, ISE supports multi-line editing that permits the insertion of blank or new lines under selected lines in the command pane. Selective execution allows developers to execute or check specific portions of the script by pointing out the desired part of the script and by pressing the Run Script or F5 button. Users can also incorporate breakpoints to test variables and script behaviors at critical points. It is supported to copy and paste the text. A context-sensitive help system gives more information on any object. The ISE itself provides several customization options, which allow users to configure text, fonts, and templates, add line and column numbers, and change keyboard shortcuts.

Further variants of the PowerShell Integrated Scripting Environment incorporate cmdlets, parameters, files, and values to autocomplete capabilities. Save the script every few minutes to prevent material loss when a crash occurs. The Snippets feature saves short code segments for reuse, and a most recent list offers quick access to recent files. PowerShell ISE merges command and output panels into one panorama to represent the PowerShell console response more closely. Users will increase PowerShell ISE's capabilities and functionality with code based on the ISE Scripting Object Model.

The table below lists the latest and updated features in Windows PowerShell ISE for this version.

IntelliSense

IntelliSense is a Windows PowerShell ISE automated completion assistance feature. IntelliSense shows the click-on menus with cmdlets, parameters, parameter values, files, or directories as you type.

With IntelliSense, it is easier to discover cmdlets and syntax when building scripts with Windows PowerShell ISE. You can also use Windows PowerShell ISE to learn how to create new scripts for Windows PowerShell.

In Windows PowerShell ISE, when you type cmdlets, a scrollable and clickable menu displays that allow you to browse and choose the commands necessary.

Snippets

PowerShell ISE comes with a default collection of snippets. Snippets are short Windows PowerShell code parts you can add to the scripts you build in Windows PowerShell ISE. By operating on Windows PowerShell ISE, you can add snippets with the New-Snippet cmdlet. You can easily compile and build scripts to automate your system with snippets.

To use Windows PowerShell 3.0 or later, select Start Snippets in the Edit Menu or press Ctrl+J.

Add-on tools

Windows PowerShell ISE also supports object model add-on software. Such add-ons are controls from the Windows Presentation Foundation (WPF) that are presented vertically or horizontally in the monitor. A tabbed control shows several add-on devices in a window. You can also add or remove tools created by non-Microsoft parties. See Windows PowerShell ISE Scripting Object Model for more detail.

Add-ons allow us to expand and customize Windows PowerShell ISE using tools that improve the scripting experience and functionality.

Windows PowerShell ISE 3.0 comes with an add-on button. The add-on commands help you to search the cmdlets by accessing the Script and Console Panes side by side support with the cmdlets.

Additional add-ons can be found on the Add-ons menu using the Open Add-on Tools button.

Restart manager and auto-save

Windows PowerShell ISE now saves your open scripts in a separate location every two minutes. When Windows PowerShell ISE restarts after an unexpected crash or reboot, scripts opened during the last session are restored even if the scripts have not been saved.

To adjust the automatic save interval, run the command $psise. Options. AutoSaveMinuteInterval in the Console pane.

Inside Windows PowerShell ISE, you can now function, knowing that your open scripts are saved automatically.

Windows PowerShell ISE 2.0 does not automatically save files.

Most-recently used list

Windows PowerShell ISE now has a list of files most commonly used. When the Windows PowerShell ISE file is opened, the file is added to the most frequently used list in the File menu.

To change the default number of files in the most recently used folder, run $psise. Options. MruCount as the command in the Console Pane. Now you can easily access your commonly used files using the most recently used list. Windows PowerShell ISE 2.0 has no new lists.

Console Pane

The different command and output panels available in the first Windows PowerShell ISE update were merged in a single window. The Control Panel is similar to a standard Windows PowerShell control, but incorporates the following upgrades:

Full Unicode support

F1 context-sensitive assistance

Ctrl+F1 context-sensitive

Show-Command

Complex script and right-to-left support

Support Font

Zoom line-select and block-select modes

Preserving typed content on the command line while pressing

UpArrow to view history oppositely. format coloring for input text (not output text), including XML syntax IntelliSense Brace matching error indicator

Adding these console pane improvements offers a more clear scripting experience with the user interface. ISE 2.0 has different input and output panes for Windows PowerShell.

Command-line switches

You can add the following new command-line switches if you launch Windows PowerShell ISE (by typing PowerShell ise.exe).

Profile: Launch Windows PowerShell ISE in multithreaded apartment mode without running $profile

Help: Displays Support window

MTA: Starting Windows PowerShell ISE. The default Windows PowerShell ISE operating mode is single-threaded apartment mode or -sta.

By adding those command-line switches, you can monitor the Windows PowerShell ISE system.

Such command-line switches can not be recognized by Windows PowerShell ISE 2.0.

New Editor Features

Specific capabilities of Windows PowerShell ISE include:

Windows PowerShell ISE now colors XML syntax in the same way as Windows PowerShell syntax colors.

Brace matching-Windows PowerShell ISE involves matching and highlighting of braces, and can be used in the following ways: (For example, the closing brace is found by using the Go to Match command or Ctrl +, where a brace is selected).

The script panel supports sketches, allowing the collapse or expansion of code sections by clicking on the left margin of the plus or minus signs. To mark the start or end of a collapsible segment, use braces or #region and #endregion tags. Press Ctrl+M to enlarge or collapse all areas.

Editing of text by drag and drop-Windows PowerShell ISE now supports the editing of text by drag and drop. You can pick any text block and drag the text to a different place in the editor or console to transfer the text. When you hold down the ctrl key when dragging the selected text, the text will be copied to the new location when you release the mouse button. In this version of Windows PowerShell ISE, the Windows PowerShell ISE tab opens when you drag and drop files to Windows PowerShell ISE.

Parse Error show-Red underlines are used to signify parse errors. If you mouse over a given mistake, the text of the tooltip shows the issue in the code.

Zoom — You can use the zoom slider (on the bottom right corner of the Windows PowerShell ISE window) or the $psise.options.Zoom command in the Console Pane to zoom the console's content percentage.

Rich copy and paste text-Copying the font, size, and color details for the original set in Windows PowerShell ISE will be preserved.

Selection of blocks-You can pick a block of text by pressing the Alt + Shift + Arrow key while selecting text on the Script Pane with your mouse.

New Help viewer window

Through clicking on F1 while your cursor is in a cmdlet or highlighting a section of a cmdlet, the new support viewer opens a context-sensitive cmdlet aid. Type operators in the console pane to see Windows PowerShell About support, and then click F1.

Download the latest version of the Windows PowerShell Help topics from the Microsoft website before using this tool. The simplest way to access the Help topics is to run Update-Help Cmdlet as an administrator in the console window.

You can change where the F1 key seeks help. You can set or clear the checkbox In the Tools / Options menu, in the General Settings tab, in the Other Settings tab, Using local support content instead of online content. Upon review, the client searches for the cmdlet aid contained in the downloaded support folder of the modules. When the checkbox is removed, the customer searches online for help.

What is the added value of this change?

Context-sensitive support offers an interactive learning experience without leaving your current script or cmdlet.

What functions otherwise?

Pressing F1 has opened the support file on your local computer in previous versions of Windows PowerShell ISE. A window opens with the aid of the cmdlet that is searchable and configurable in Windows PowerShell ISE 3.0. For Windows PowerShell ISE 3.0, and for Windows PowerShell 3.0, this support experiment is new.

Uses of PowerShell ISE

The Windows PowerShell ISE is an editing tool for creating, modifying, checking, and executing PowerShell scripts in Windows environments. The ISE provides a more immersive and versatile platform than a typical PowerShell console.

Save time and popular scripting errors. Long sequences of the multiple command lines are commonly used in scripts with granular parameters. In PowerShell and PowerShell

ISE, it is possible to create the same script. Still, ISE features such as an interactive index of existing commands make it easy to locate important commands, pick appropriate parameters in the pane, and drop the correctly formatted command. This can save time together with other editing niceties by speeding up the correct command layout and reducing common typing and syntax errors, which can take time to find and repair.

Boost debugging and research files. A script is a short piece of software with instructions for the scripting language PowerShell. Like any program, the script is bound to produce bugs, surveillance, and unintended consequences. ISE features such as a built-in debugger can help identify common errors and suggest corrections before the script is executed. Additional features such as breakpoints and selective implementation allow developers to test the desired portions of the script and intentionally interrupt the execution at critical points to check the status of significant variables and other behaviors.

Read more about specific scripts. Scripts may be extremely interactive structures, in which a script communicates with other scripts. This can lead to complicated relations with vanilla engines like PowerShell, which can be difficult to follow. The ISE supports multiple simultaneous running environments, which allow developers to load and simultaneously monitor the cause-and-effect relationships between several scripts. The ISE helps with troubleshooting, especially when one script changes trigger an unwanted action or error in another.

PowerShell vs. PowerShell ISE

Both PowerShell and PowerShell ISE provide the same basic scripting capabilities for Windows environments. The main difference between the two is comfort. PowerShell is a simpler and easier scripting and running environment, while ISE offers a more versatile and efficient editing and execution capabilities. PowerShell can be a good platform for simple tasks that are straightforward actions. The ISE is suitable for massive, complex, and interrelated scripting tasks.

A word processor contrast offers a simple analogy. A device like Notepad is suitable for making and editing notes and short, quick texts. But a method like Word has much more editing functions, fonts, colors, formatting and orthography, and grammar tests. Word could, therefore, be a suitable method for complex tasks, such as writing technical reports and designing a book chapter. Nonetheless, both devices are word processors.

Advantages of PowerShell ISE

If you have been using Windows PowerShell for some time, you already know how valuable it is to work with information from a wide range of sources. Nevertheless, sometimes PowerShell's shell can look pretty clunky, if not entirely irritating. Simple operations like copying, pasting, and transferring code lines can transform into complex procedures that are often more complicated than scratching the code.

To address the weakness of the command tube, developers often use a second program simultaneously with PowerShell. For example, you could use a Text Editing function of Notepad to prepare the code before pasting it into a console window or a Notepad++ source code editor to allow the use of more features, such as Auto-completion, multi-document tabs and the syntax outline regions. However helpful, you always switch between multiple connections to get the job done. This is where the

Integrated Scripting Environment (ISE) PowerShell comes in. The ISE PowerShell is a host program for writing and editing your scripts in a text editor, and executing your scripts in a command shell. The PowerShell ISE gives you the simplicity of both worlds in a single graphic environment that is easy to use and provides many extras, including coloring the code, debugging context-sensitive assistance, and much more.

However, be mindful that not all ISE versions are equivalent. PowerShell ISE 2.0 was launched shortly after PowerShell 2.0 was launched. ISE 2.0 provides basic functionality but is a wall-down version compared to what ISE is today.

PowerShell ISE 3.0 was released, which contains several features that are now available as ISE drawing cards, including auto-save, samples, IntelliSense, and additional tools. Because ISE 2.0 lacks so many of the features, I will focus only on version 3.0. Yet note, PowerShell ISE 4.0 is just around the corner. Microsoft plans to ship it with Windows 8.1 and Windows Server 2012 R2 — along with PowerShell 4.0. (To see the TechNet article "Windows PowerShell Integrated Scripting Environment (ISE)" for a list of Windows OSs and their default versions, see

TechNet). Based on what I've seen so far, it does not seem to be any significant change between PowerShell ISE 3.0 and PowerShell ISE 4.0 interferences.

Disadvantages Of Powershell ISE

One of Windows PowerShell's potential downsides is that it is object-based. With most shells, you use text-based commands to do the job in the writing of scripts. If you turn from another shell to Windows PowerShell, you will have to adapt to a different way of thinking. This may be a problem that takes time for some users to get through.

Security Risks

Another potential downside of using Windows PowerShell is that it can pose some possible security risks. Many IT professionals use it as a way of connecting to other computers and servers remotely. PowerShell can leave some holes open for security breaches when engaging in this process. This creates the potential for the installation of viruses, malware, or other dangerous programs on the server. If someone else knows about Windows PowerShell, it might cause problems.

Web Server

Another problem with Windows PowerShell is that when you use remote features, you need to run a Web server on your computer. It takes an extra room on a file. In many instances, businesses will not want to take up more space on their servers and allocate more money for that. You may need to obtain approval from a higher professional before that is permitted if you are an IT professional working for a company.

Considerations

Windows PowerShell has some possible disadvantages, but it also has other benefits. When Microsoft evolves it, for example, it is slowly integrated into Microsoft products and services. Windows PowerShell is versatile and easy to operate once the basics are mastered. You can also execute certain commands which are only intended to run on local networks if the remote communication function is used.

The Powershell ISE Interface

While there are some possible disadvantages for Windows PowerShell, there are certain benefits. For example, as Microsoft develops it, it is slowly incorporated into

Microsoft products and services. Windows PowerShell is versatile and easy to manage when you know everything. It also allows you to execute commands which are only meant to be performed on local networks with the remote link feature. This pane is the code editor where PowerShell scripts are written and debugged. In this window, you can also run scripts or parts of scripts. (Although you run them from the scripting panel, PowerShell runs them in the console panel and shows these results in that panel.) However, the current script files can be opened and modified.

Pane Controller. The Pane Console is like a PowerShell command tube. You may insert commands directly into the Console Pane, execute them, and view the results shown in the Console Pane. (Note that you can also enter and execute Script Pane commands, but the results will also be shown in the Console Pane.) Tools Pane. This pane can be used to use additional tools. By default, the PowerShell ISE contains the other commands, which will be shown automatically when you open it in the add-on tools window.

The three panes in the ISE window of PowerShell. The script pane is at the top, the console pane at the base, and the tools pane is at the right side of the file. However, by choosing the appropriate option in the View menu, you can monitor if and where the panels are displayed. More options for viewing add-ons are included in the Add-ons menu. The PowerShell ISE window also contains several other menus and management and editing tools for your PowerShell scripts, which are mostly self-explainable.

The Script and Console Panes have a single PowerShell key. Just one PowerShell tab is shown when you open the PowerShell ISE. Nevertheless, you can open additional PowerShell tabs and open Script and Console Panes within each tab. The PowerShell ISE window, for example, includes three PowerShell tables, with one tab active. The script pane will contain multiple tabs, each with its script file. For instance, in the script pane, there are four files opened, and every script file is allocated to its tab. The Console Pane reveals part of the output of the first script file executing the commands. If you run a command in one of the other script windows, these results will be inserted after the current control panel results, except if you delete the button. (All script tabs in a PowerShell tab share a specific Pane Console.) Though, the Console Pane would be an instance of its own if you were going to use a particular PowerShell tab and pointing to either the local computer or a remote one. In other words, each PowerShell tab can be thought of as a link to a certain device. This machine is the local one by default.

Customizing The Powershell ISE Interface

The PowerShell ISE offers a range of interface customization options. You can use the Tools menu and press Options to access these options. When the Options dialog box is shown, the Colors and Fonts tab is opened, the colors and font in the Script and Console Panes can be identified here. In terms of how you want to color different language elements in the Script and Console Panes, you'll find you can be quite precise.

You can also choose a theme that sets the color and font settings. This means that you have to set colors individually if a theme meets your requirements.

Whatever method you use to pick the colors, you can immediately apply your adjustments once you have made your selections. These adjustments should then, in principle, begin when you restart PowerShell ISE. Sadly, when you pick background colors for the Console Pane, PowerShell ISE is a little unstable. You can see that the background color isn't quite what you planned when you restart PowerShell ISE. For this purpose, you may want to use a script to change the settings and save the script to one of the files in your profile. For example, to adjust the background color of the Console pane, use the following script: $psISE.Options. ConsolePaneBackgroundColor= "white." This script calls the Options property of the $psISE variable. The built-in variable PowerShell returns Microsoft. PowerShell. Host. ISE.ObjectModelRoot property. The object Options property lets you access the different options that monitor PowerShell ISE window appearance and behavior. In this case, you access and set its value to white with the ConsolePaneBackgroundColor option.

You$psISE.Options When you understand how to use $psISE.Options to configure the PowerShell ISA code, you might still want your settings to be modified so that they are used automatically when you start the PowerShell ISE. Yet note that not all PowerShell ISE profile files are the same as PowerShell's command shell. You may need to build and update files separately from the standard profile files. By running the command, you can easily obtain a list of current settings and their values.

You may set up several other settings on the General Settings tab of the Settings dialog box in addition to configuring the colors and fonts used on the PowerShell ISE. You can customize the actions of the Script Pane, IntelliSense, and other elements of the PowerShell ISE window here. Alternatively, you can customize certain settings using the $psISE—options property.

Scripting In The Powershell ISE

Let's get to the PowerShell ISE fun part, the actual scripting. Though many of the editing functions are available in both the script and console panes, most administrators will smile from the script pane. You can do everything from there, like running a whole or part of a script. That said, the Console Pane is still a lot to like.

One enjoyable function of both sides is context-sensitive assistance. You only need to place your cursor in a cmdlet text and press F1 to access the functionality. This opens a separate window with information about the cmdlet, including its syntax, supporting parameters, and examples of the cmdlet in practice. For example, the help file is shown for the cmdlet Get-Service. If you scroll down this pane, in addition to what is shown in the figure, you will find numerous specifics about the cmdlet.

However, remember that the context-sensitive assistance program doesn't always function. Suppose you are making a description of the foreach control flow. The Support file for the ForEach-Object Cmdlet will be showing the method if you place your cursor in the foreach keyword, not the foreach control flow statement. In most instances, however, the feature works well. It can save you a lot of time by getting the right details if you need it.

Another great feature of PowerShell ISE is IntelliSense, an auto finish window that appears when starting to type the cmdlet name, parameter, parameter value, file, or folder. What is shown depends on your command sense.

When the IntelliSense window opens, you can easily scroll into your script into the PowerShell language feature you are searching for. For starters, the window IntelliSense appears when you type get-s. In this case, three cmdlets are available to choose from. If one of the cmdlets is the one you want, you pick it and paste it into your script automatically.

It's helpful to know the colors that are used in PowerShell ISE for various types of language components, for example, the many different colors that are used in the Script Pane in Figure 7. Commands are white, red variables, blue cmdlets, and so forth. The Console Pane often displays color linguistic elements when you first type them into your script–before you run your code. Then all goes back to the base hue. The colors shown in Figure 7 are the default PowerShell ISE settings, but you can change them to match your preferences, as mentioned earlier.

You may have noted that the Script pane includes regions often known as outline views. Regions are the parts of code that have been followed by a vertical line, and a plus or minus sign is at the top of the line. When you click on the symbol, this section of code will collapse or extend. For example, the #region tag begins, and the #endregion tag ends. All in that area will collapse into a single line, which can be extended at any time. Regions in the Script Pane are only visible.

The PowerShell ISE supports two regions: user-defined and system-set regions (i.e. PowerShell ISE regions). The user-defined areas begin with the tag #region and end with the tag #endregion. You just add the tags and enter any other information after the tag. Administrators typically include only #region tag information. The first #region, for example, contains label variables.

Besides user-defined areas, PowerShell ISE automatically determines regions for curly brackets expressions, which are included in statements like if and foreach. Two system-set regions can be seen. The first starts immediately below the first line of the if statement (line 12). The second one begins directly below the first line of the forecast (line 17). As shown in this example, regions can be combined. How when the systems-set regions collapse appear.

As you can see, regions offer an easy way to view the big picture of your script and make sure the meaning is valid. You only click on the plus sign to redevelop any of the regions. Another useful aspect of PowerShell ISE is a set of snippets— PowerShell code short pieces that you can use to build your scripts as models. You can even add to the list your excerpts.

You place your cursor where you want to insert the code and press Ctrl+J to add a snippet to a file. It lists the available snippets in a pop-up window. The list can then be scrolled, the snippet you want picked and the code displayed. The code for the do-while fragment, for example. To insert code into your file, double-click on the snippet in the pop-up window. The fundamental components of the argument are added. Now let's look at one more aspect of PowerShell ISE scripting. As noted earlier, the command add-on comes in with PowerShell ISE and is presented in the Add-on Tools Pane. Notice that the add-on commands lists all PowerShell commands available. You can access the list by searching for commands based on a particular module, name, or both.

The commands add-on does more than list the commands available. If you select a specific command, options for building, running, inserting, and copying will be given. In this case, the cmdlet Get-Service is chosen. Note that three tabs are shown. Each tab corresponds to the cmdlet's syntax type. You may pick or assign parameters within each window. In other words, if you do not know a certain order, or if you are new to PowerShell entirely, you have a graphical interface for constructing commands, which is especially useful. You can execute, insert it in the Console Pane once you have created your instruction, or copy it to be stored wherever you want.

Debugging Scripts In The Powershell ISE

PowerShell ISE offers a set of tools for debugging the code in the script pane. Essentially, in your script, you set one or more breakpoints and execute the script. If the processor reaches the first point of interruption, it stops before you start. At every breakpoint, the values stored in the variables can be checked until you hit the breakpoint. This can help ensure that the structure of your code works as intended and that the variable values are what you want them to be.

To set a breakpoint, place your cursor on the line where you want to avoid executing your code. Then right-click on the line and Toggle Breakpoint. In this case, there have been two breakpoints: one on line 18 and one on line 26. When you press F 5 now, the script will start running and run until it hits the first breakpoint. Any lines formed as breakpoints are highlighted. The highlight will change colors at this moment. Then[DBG] is followed by the cursor in the Console Pane to indicate that you are on debugging mode, and you're getting the message were to enter the breakpoint. To keep the script going, click again on F5, and PowerShell ISE picks up where it has been left off. It will run until the next breakpoint is reached.

Nevertheless, if a breakpoint such as the foreach statement is inserted into a control flow statement, the script will stop at the same breakpoint until each object in the list is routed through. If you, for example, look at the Console window, you will see that the script stopped at the same interval four times, showing that the initial foreach set contains four objects ($svcs1). The script started at line 26 to the next breakpoint, where the script was interrupted. Once you reach a breakpoint, at that time, you will search for any element. You only need to hover your cursor over a variable name, and the current values are shown. The PowerShell ISE shows the contents of the $svcs2 variable, which are the services not operating. If you looked at the contents of the $svc variable, you would only find the name of one operation.

The World Of The Powershell ISE

The PowerShell ISE has several features that can be used to ease development efforts. This tool also supports more features, including brace matching, error indicator, Unicode support, zooming ability, and the ability to save open scripts automatically.

Although I have only touched on PowerShell ISE, you should be aware of the potential of the PowerShell ISE. Because Microsoft provides the PowerShell ISE free of charge, you have little to lose if you try it out. And you could even find that you have a lot to gain.

How To Run Powershell ISE

Windows PowerShell ISE is also used in Windows 10, 8.1, 8.0 and 7, and 2008 R2 SP1 and later on Windows Server. On a Windows 10 PC, the ISE can be started by pressing Start, expands the Windows PowerShell folder in the Start menu, and then choose the Windows PowerShell ISE. After the launch of an ISE, the user may typically use ISE.

Use the pane of the screen. Once the ISE begins, it functions just like PowerShell, and users can type commands into the pane— the large, dark blue GUI field— as if they were PowerShell. For example, to run a command, type the command on the command prompt into the console pane, and press Enter. By using Shift+Enter— a line return— between commands, users can enter and execute multiple commands. Users can stop running a command on the GUI via the Stop Operation button or on the keyboard by using Ctrl+Break.

Building and using tabs. Up to 32 simultaneous yet separate running environments or sessions are provided by the

PowerShell ISE 2.0. The growing environment is called a window, and users can switch between tabs—Tap New PowerShell Tab on the File menu to create a new tab. Users can choose to build and use a remote PowerShell tab to log in onto remote computers, although additional details are required for logging in and accessing remote computers.

Manage to debug breakpoints. The ISE encourages the use of breakpoints in the script in which a manual analysis of variables and environments is avoided. Once a breaking point has occurred, the user will execute commands to test the script status, adjust the script status, and even restart its operation. Users can use line breakpoints to pause, to variable breakpoints to pause when the desired variable shifts, and to pause when the desired command is identified. The ISE allows users to set, delete, and disable interruptions.

Run a profile at the beginning of the ISE. A profile is a script that begins at the start of the session. A profile can be important to customize the PowerShell ISE environment for the aliases, functions, variables, colors and font settings and other ISE session or tab preferences. Users can create, pick, edit, and disable ISE profiles.

Write scripts and run them. The ISE is primarily used to write, modify and run PowerShell scripts in Windows. Script files can include regular script (.ps1), data script (.psd1), script module files (.psm1) as well as files such as.ps1xml configuration files, XML files and text files. Script files may also be included. Click New on the toolbar to create a new script file, or on the File menu, click New. The new empty file is shown in a new tab. Users can add script commands and info. To run the script, on the toolbar press Execute Script or the File menu, click Execute. To run only one part of the script, pick or highlight the desired part of the script and then press Execute Selection from the File menu or click Execute Selection from the toolbar.

Microsoft Support And Replacement

Windows PowerShell v2 implemented the PowerShell Integrated Scripting Environment first. The ISE has been revised for PowerShell v3 and improved. ISE is supported in all versions of Windows PowerShell up to version 5.1 as of February 2020. It is important to note that ISE is no longer active. Although ISE still is supported by safety and practical updates, ISE for PowerShell v6 or later is not revised. In favor of alternative platforms such as the Visual Studio Code with the PowerShell Expand, PowerShell v6 and later users that choose to forgo ISE through the Visual Studio Marketplace.

Reasons For Using Powershell ISE Instead Of The Powershell Console

Windows has a PowerShell command-line interface that suits this powerful language even better. By the way, this post explains how to make ISE tile visible if you can't find Power Shell ISE on your Start Screen. Many administrators believe that the integrated scripting environment for Windows PowerShell is only for writing scripts. Perhaps the explanation is that the "Integrated Development Environment" sounds a little like "Eye." And when they need a console PowerShell, the old-style "Windows 95 DOS prompt" is released. The PowerShell ISE is a fantastic scripting tool, but it's a good CLI as well. You may reduce or decrease the size of the script editor and then have a very nice PowerShell console. Below, I list some reasons why PowerShell ISE should be your primary CLI.

Copy commands ^

Have you ever tried to copy a PowerShell prompt command that's longer than one line? I don't know who had the idea that labeling text as a block could be useful rather than choosing it to the line by line. I never recall that I need such an odd way to choose an email. I also don't know of a way to pick text without a mouse on the screen. You can mark the text as in any editor in the PowerShell ISE, i.e., line by line and by using the SHIFT + cursor keys. The text you use with CTRL+C can be copied.

Paste commands ^

Pasting on the screen is also somewhat uncomfortable. Right-click is the quickest way (if Quick Edit mode is activated), but real PowerShell geeks avoid clicking whenever possible. ALT+SPACE+E+P is not a convenient option. You can only paste with CTRL+V in PowerShell ISE as normal. However, much more importantly, my clipboard history tool, ClipX, works in PowerShell ISE. It is only half as efficient to scroll through previous commands since all your previous commands look at ClipX. Notice that you need to execute ClipX with admin privileges if you want to use ClipX with a higher PowerShell ISE console.

Editing ^

I always find it very useful to have a PowerShell ISE editor right at hand. Often, when I play with a long command, I retain and copy different versions of the command and paste them to the PowerShell ISE prompt. I also often start a command directly from the PowerShell ISE by pressing F5. I try to avoid mistakes wherever I can. If I have several editor versions of the instruction, I pick a particular line and press F8. It is also possible to execute part of a command in the editor by labeling the component and then pressing F8.

Switch to scripting ^

The things I want to do are often not as easy as I thought. I also find it. Piping is enjoyable, but you sometimes get to a point where you know you're better off writing a little script. Since my experiments already include the majority of the commands in my editor, I can easily switch from CLI to scripting. I don't think there is a true difference between CLI and scripting. A command is just a single line file.

Window size ^

One of the worst drawbacks of the PowerShell prompt is that you cannot merely extend the window using a mouse; you only get a window with several lines specified in the window properties if you click on the complete screen symbol. The PowerShell ISE pane, by comparison, resizes as a standard Windows program. PowerShell commands are usually very long and easier to read and edit if you can hold them without a line break on one line.

Context sensitive help ^

The context-sensitive support is a handy feature of the PowerShell ISE Editor. When you start typing, a small window will appear, which shows the cmdlets matching the text entered. So if you don't know the exact cmdlet name, you can start typing and then scroll through all the options. Also very useful is that when you click-," "PowerShell ISE will show you the available parameters after entering the name of the cmdlet. You even get a list of possible choices after completing the parameter. This works only in the editor, not in the CLI of PowerShell ISE. But it is not a problem as you can start the command with F5 from the editor only, rather than pressing Enter.

Command Add-on ^

Clicking on the Add-on command in the PowerShell ISE toolbar will reveal a sidebar to the right where you can check for cmdlets. You can also confine your quest to a particular module.

Syntax highlighting ^

PowerShell ISE also supports highlighting, syntax, of course. This helps to avoid syntax errors and makes it easier to read your order until shot.

Tabs ^

The PowerShell ISE tabs are helpful if you operate concurrently on several administrative tasks. I consider it much easier than dealing with multiple windows of the PowerShell console. You have your editor for each window.

Zoom ^

You will find that it narrowed your eyes a lot if you work a lot with PowerShell. Coders are the best customers of an eye doctor. If you have been working on the CLI all day and you clearly can not see the syntax mistake, you can prefer your eyes and widen fonts. You can zoom with the mouse wheel, as with any other Windows program, by pressing the CTRL-key. CTRL+ can also be zoomed to increase the font size and CTRL to minimize font size. This works in the PowerShell ISE editor and CLI.

POWERSHELL CONCEPTS

The best way to start with PowerShell is to check out the home page of Windows PowerShell.

The home page URL of Windows PowerShell is http:/www.microsoft.com / PowerShell/.

This website is an excellent resource for PowerShell information and helps you to download documents, tools, read news from companies, and get the latest PowerShell versions. Download and install PowerShell is your next move. It is important to clarify before plunging into the installation process, which version of PowerShell is most appropriate for your requirements. PowerShell 1.0 and PowerShell 2.0 CTP2 are currently available for download from Microsoft. The following sections describe each of these variants.

The home page of Microsoft Windows PowerShell,

PowerShell 1.0 RTW

The current version of PowerShell is version 1.0 RTW (Release To Web) as of this writing. This PowerShell version was released in November 2006. Although PowerShell 1.0 RTW does not include the new PowerShell

2.0 CTP2 features, "The PowerShell update is the only version that can be recommended for use in a production environment. PowerShell 1.0 RTW can be downloaded from the following URL for all compatible platforms: http://www.microsoft.com/windowsserver2003/technologies/management/powershell/download.mspx.

Enabling PowerShell 1.0 on Windows Server 2008

Windows PowerShell 1.0 is included as an operating system option for Windows Server 2008. Nonetheless, it must be implemented via the ServerManager snap-in before PowerShell can be used. Follow these steps to complete this task:

Sign in to the appropriate server with the privileges of the local administrator.

Click Start, then click Execute.

Type ServerManager.msc in the Run dialog box, and then select OK.

Click the Add Features option in the Features Summary portion.

Select the Windows PowerShell option and click Next on the Select Options tab.

Select the choices on the Confirm Configuration Choices tab, check, and click Install.

See the results on the Deployment Results page and click Close.

PowerShell 2.0 CTP2

PowerShell 2.0 CTP2 is a PowerShell language Community Technology Preview edition. This version of PowerShell 2.0 has the new language features and is best suited for those of us who want to play with the PowerShell 2.0's new capabilities in a lab or pre-production environment. You have to ensure that your device meets the following minimum installation criteria before installing PowerShell 2.0 CTP2:

Windows XP with Service Pack 1, Windows Vista with Servicepack 1, Windows Server 2003 with Service Pack 1, and Windows Server 2008 are supported for PowerShell 2.0 CTP2 operating systems.

Microsoft. NET Framework 2.0 is needed for PowerShell 2.0 CTP2 installation.

Microsoft enables the new Graphical PowerShell and Out-Gridview cmdlets in PowerShell 2.0 CTP2. NET Framework 3.0.

The cmdlet Get-Event runs on Windows Vista and Windows Server 2008 only and includes Microsoft. NET Framework 3.5.

The CTP2 feature of Windows Remote Management (WinRM) is necessary for PowerShell 2.0 CTP2 to use the new remote functions.

Remote works only with Service Pack 1 (SP1) and Windows Server 2008 in Windows Vista.

Before Installing PowerShell 2.0 CTP2

If PowerShell 1.0 is currently installed on your device, you must delete it before PowerShell 2.0 is installed. The following steps identify the procedures to uninstall PowerShell 1.0 according to your OS.

Uninstalling Windows PowerShell 1.0

Windows XP-SP2 and Windows Server 2003: Select the option to view updates under Add / Remove Programs. Disable updates for your device from PowerShell, as applicable: KB926139 (en-us), KB926140 (localized), and KB926141 (MUI pack).

Windows Vista: Go to Control Panel > Programs and Features> Updates installed. Uninstall the update to PowerShell: KB928439.

Windows Server 2008: PowerShell 1.0 is an optional feature in Windows Server 2008. If PowerShell 1.0 is allowed, you must turn off it before installing PowerShell 2.0 CTP2. Launch the Server Manager and select the feature removal option. Pick from the list PowerShell and disable the functions.

The Microsoft Download Center

Install And Configure Winrm (Windows Remote Management)

WinRM is Microsoft's WS-Management Protocol, a Simple Object Access Protocol (SOAP) protocol that provides a common method for access to management knowledge and sharing systems. WinRM uses ports 80 and 443 by design and is compatible with most firewalls. Nevertheless, WinRM also permits the modification of these default ports if necessary. WinRM is native to the Windows Vista & Windows Server 2008, but the WS-Management 2.0 CTP feature is included in the PowerShell 2.0 CTP2 update to allow remote control. Y

Downloading and Installing PowerShell 2.0

After the installation of the.NET Framework 2.0 and.NET Framework 3.0, you can download the PowerShell 2.0 CTP2 software kit from your server after verification that all WinRM components are installed on your device.

Download Windows PowerShell 2.0

For installing PowerShell, you can find the correct PowerShell installation kit for Windows version x86 or x64 on the download page. Then click the correct download link to download the PowerShell installation kit. Next, launch the installation of PowerShell by double-clicking on Open on the download window. (The filename differs according to the platform, version of the Windows and the language pack.) Follow the installation instructions after you have started the installer. Another way is to quietly install the command line with the PowerShell installation file name via the /quiet switch. When you plan to install PowerShell on many various systems and want to distribute your installation using a logon file, system management server (SMD), or other software management tool, this installation method can be useful. Follow these steps to carry out a silent installation:

Click Start > Run.

Type cmd, and then click OK to open a cmd command prompt.

Type PowerShell-exe-filename /quiet (replacing the italicized text with the PowerShell installation filename) and press Enter.

You can access it by three different methods after downloading PowerShell. To use the first method from the Start menu, follow the following steps:

Click Start > All Programs > Windows PowerShell 2.0.

Click Windows PowerShell.

To make use of the second method, follow these steps:

Click Start > Run.

Type PowerShell in the Run dialog box, and then click OK.

Both steps open the PowerShell console.

The PowerShell console

Follow these steps to use the third cmd command prompt method:

Click Start > Run.

Type cmd and click OK to open a cmd command prompt.

At the command prompt, type powershell, as shown in Figure 2.5, and press Enter.

The PowerShell console has been opened by cmd.

Configure WSMan Settings

The PowerShell Remoting and PSJobs features depend on Windows Remote Management (WinRM) technology, as described above. A variety of configuration changes need to be made to the default WSMan settings in PowerShell 2.0. This method is luckily made more accessible by using a PowerShell script called Configure-Wsman.ps1 in the $pshome folder. This script configures the settings for WS-Man. The command Configure-WSMan.ps1 executes the following from the $pshome location:

& $pshome\Configure-Wsman.ps1

Note: Due to the default script implementation policy of PowerShell 2.0 (initially restrained), the Configure-Wyman.ps1 script is initially not allowed to run. The following screenshot illustrates the error you get if you try to run this script without changing the default script execution policy.

PS   C:\>&$pshome\Configure-Wsman.ps1   File C:\WINDOWS\system32\WindowsPowerShell\v1.0\Confi gure-Wsman.ps1 can not be accessed as scripting on that system is disabled. For more information, see "get-help about signing."To line:1 char:2+ & < < < < < $pshome\Configure-Wsman.ps1PS C:\ > To enable the successful execution of a Configure-WSMan.ps1 script, the Set-ExecutionPolicy cmdlet can be used to set a RemoteSigned Execution Policy, as shown in the following example. Once the script is done, the cmdlet of Set-ExecutionPolicy can optionally be used to return PowerShell to its default execution policy. The following command sequence shows three separate actions: RemoteSigned setting of the script execution policy, Configure-WSMan.ps1 script execution, then Default setting of the script execution policy. The next screenshot shows a shorter version of the verbose output created by running Configure-WSMan.ps1. (We use the Set-ExecutionPolicy cmdlet again later in this chapter when we write a simple PowerShell script.' Understanding PowerShell Security talks more in-depth about PowerShell security and related best practices.)

PS C: > RemoteSignedPS C:\ > & $pshoma\Configure-Wsman.ps1Configure WSMan. Configure WSMan CompleteSignedPS port 80 and port 443PS C:\ > DefaultPS C:\ > After the steps mentioned above have been completed, PowerShell 2.0 CTP2 is configured and ready to be used.

Understanding The Command-Line Interface (CLI)

The CLI PowerShell syntax is identical to that for other CLI shells. Naturally, the basic feature of the PowerShell command is the name of the executable program. Also, parameters and arguments for parameters can be used to define the function. A PowerShell command can, therefore, have the following formats:

[command name][command name] -[parameter][command name] -[parameter] –[parameter] [argument1][command name] -[parameter] –[parameter] [argument1],[argument2]

You can see an example of using a command, a parameter and an argument, by executing the dir command, with a / w parameter and a C:\temp*.txt argument, shown here:[C:\>dir/w C:\temp*.txt Volume on drive C, OS Volume Serial Number is 1784-ADF9 directory of C:\tempBad Stuff.txt mediapc.txt note.txt 4 File(s) 953 bytes file(s) The findings are different if you use the dir command without any parameters or arguments. PowerShell achieves the same result. For example, here is a simple PowerShell command that provides information about exploring.exe processes: PS C:\ > get-process—Name of exploring NP M(K) WS(K) WS(K) CPU(s) Name of the process I d of explorerPS C:\ > The following example is Get-Process. In this instance, the command—-name is the parameter, and the explorer is the argument of the argument:\ > In this example, Get-Process is the command, the name of the parameter is the explorer, and the explorer is the argument. This command results in process information on explorer.exe. If no parameters or arguments are used, the Get-Process command only lists information from all processes currently running, not information from a particular process. You must understand the syntax of the command if you are to regulate what a command does or do more than its default action. Use the Get-Help function, addressed later in "Useful Cmdlets," to use commands in the CLI easily to obtain detailed information about what command does and what command needs to be used.

Tab Key Auto-Completion In Powershell

Like the cmd command prompt, PowerShell immediately completes file and directory names. While PowerShell returns the first file or directory name in the current directory if you enter a partial file or directory name and press TAB. Pressing Tab returns a second match and helps you to loop through the results list. Just like the cmd prompt, the auto-completion key for PowerShell can also be automatically completed on wildcards, as shown in this example, PS C:\ > cd C:\Doc* < tab> PS C:\ > cd' C:\Documents and Settings ' PS C:\Documents and Settings > The difference between the auto-completion of Tab key in cmd and PowerShell is that PowerShell can auto-complete the controls in this case. For example, a partial command name can be entered, and the tab key can be pressed. Powershell steps can also be used in a list of possible command matches: PS C:\ > Get-Pro < Tab> PS C:\ > Get-Prozess The PowerShell parameter associated with a particular command can also be automatically completed. Just enter a command name and partial parameter name and press the Tab key and the PowerShell loop through the command parameters you specified. This approach also works for command-related variables. PowerShell also automatically completes the methods and properties of variables and objects. Take an example with a variable called "$Z" set to the value "Variable": PS C:\ > $Z= "Variable" PS C:\ > $Z.<tab > PowerShell loops through the possibility to perform operations against the $Z variable when you type $Z and click the tab key. For example, if you select the property for $Z.Length and click Enter, PowerShell will return the string length in the variant for $Z., as shown in this section: PS C:\ > $Z= Variable PS C:\ > $Z.<tab > PS C:\ > $Z.Length8PS C:\ Properties are mentioned without an open parenthesis (such as in the previous example $Z.Length) and methods are listed with an open parenthesis, as in this example shown: PS C:\ > $Z= PS C:\ > $Z.con <tab > PS C:\ > $Z.Contains(if $Z.Contains(prompt is displayed), you can use this method to check whether the $Z variable contains character V by type: PS C:\ > $Z= "V$" This feature is mostly aesthetic since PowerShell is not case sensitive by design.

Greater Visibility Through PowerShell Logging
Installation
No software updates are required to support enhanced PowerShell logging in Windows 10.

PowerShell is updated to allow improved logging in PowerShell 5.0 (recommended) for Windows 7/8.1/2008/2012:
.NET 4.5

Windows Management Framework (WMF) 4.0 (Windows 7/2008 only)

Windows Management Framework (WMF) 5.0

Once WMF 5.0 is enabled, Windows 7 and 2008 R2 must be updated to Windows Management Framework (WMF) 4.0.

For Windows 7/8.1/2008/2012, allowing improved logging in PowerShell 4.0 requires:

» .NET 4.5
» Windows Management Framework (WMF) 4.0
» The appropriate WMF 4.0 update
  - 8.1/2012 R2 – KB3000850
  - 2012 – KB3119938
  - 7/2008 R2 SP1 – KB3109118

Microsoft can require the completion of an automated request process to download these updates.

Logging Configuration

PowerShell supports three types of logging: logging module, logging block script, and transcription. PowerShell events are written to Microsoft-Windows-PowerShell 4Operational.evtx Operational Log.

Module Logging

The logging module records pipeline execution information as per PowerShell, including initialization of the variable and invocations. The logging module will record portions of scripts, deconfused code, and some output data. This log will collect certain data that other PowerShell logging sources have missed, although the commands executed may not be collected accurately. After PowerShell 3.0, module logging has been available. Logging events for the module are written to Event ID 4103.

While module logging produces a large volume for events (these events record useful performance, not recorded by other sources when the famous Invoke-Mimikatz script is executed, produced 2,285 events, resulting in 7 MB of the log during testing).

To allow the logging module:

Sets "Switch on Module Logging" in the "Windows PowerShell" GPO settings to allow.

In the "Tools" window, press the Name module button.

Enter* in the Names module window to record all modules.

An Optional: Mention them here to log only different modules.

Click "Okay" in the "Modul Names" window. (Note: this is not recommended.)

Click "Yes" in the "Logging Module" pane.

The following registry values would alternatively have the same effect:

»
HKLM\SOFTWARE\Wow6432Node\Policies\Microsoft\
Windows\PowerShell\ModuleLogging   →
EnableModuleLogging = 1

»
HKLM\SOFTWARE\Wow6432Node\Policies\Microsoft\
Windows\PowerShell\ModuleLogging \ModuleNames → *
= *

Script block logging

Code blocks the recording of code blocks when run by the PowerShell engine, thereby collecting the full output of a code and command code of an attacker. It also records de-fused code, because of the existence of the script block logging. Examples: in addition to documenting the original fused text, the block script log records the decoded commands passed with a the-EncodedCommand argument of PowerShell as well as the commands fused with XOR, Base64, ROT13, encryption, etc. Code block logging won't record the executed code output. EID 4104 documents script block logging events. Script blocks that surpass an event log message's maximum length are broken into multiple entries. A script is available for script file logs and broken blocks to be recompiled.

If the contents of a package matche in a list of questionable commands or scripting techniques, PowerShell 5.0 will automatically log code blocks if they are not accessible in PowerShell 4.0, even if script block logging is not allowed. Such suspect blocks are logged at the EID 4104 stage of "alert," unless the logging of scripts is expressly deactivated. This function guarantees that certain forensic data have been registered for suspicious activity even if logging is not allowed, but is not considered by Microsoft to be a security feature. Activating script block logging records all the action, not just those blocks that the PowerShell method considers suspect. It allows researchers to recognize the full range of attacker behavior. Blocks considered not to be suspicious are also logged to EID 4104 but at the levels of "verbose" and "data."

Logging script block produces fewer events than logging module (Invoke-Mimikatz generates 116 events totaling 5 MB) and records useful SIEM or log monitoring application alert indicators.

Community Policy also includes an option to "start/stop events for log script block execution." This alternative records the beginning and end of scripts in EIDs 4105 and 4106, by script block ID. This alternative may provide additional forensic details, as in the case of the long-run PowerShell script, but produces an unnecessarily large number of events (96.458 events totaling 50 MB per Invoke-Mimikatz execution) and is not appropriate for most environments.

Enabling script block logging: set "Switch on PowerShell Script Block Logging" to allow GPO settings in "Windows PowerShell."

Setting the following registry value will require logging in alternatively:»

HKLM\SOFTWARE\Wow6432Node\Policies\Microsoft\ Windows\PowerShell\ScriptBlockLogging= 1

Transcription

Transcription creates a unique record of each PowerShell session, including all input and output, just as the session happens. Transcripts are sent to user and client text files. To order to help review, transcripts also provide timestamps and metadata for each instruction. However, the transcription only records the contents of the executed scripts or output written for other purposes, such as the file system, which are shown in the PowerShell terminal. Automatic names for PowerShell transcripts avoid crashes, with names starting with "PowerShell transcript." The transcripts are written to the document folder of the user by default but can be installed in any accessible location on the local system and network. The best practice is to write transcripts to a remote network share so that defenders can read and delete data easily. Transcripts can be compressed quickly (less than six kB per Invoke-Mimikatz run) and can be checked using standard tools such as grep.

To allow transcription: set "Switch on PowerShell Transcription" to activate in "Windows PowerShell" settings.

Check the' Call headers included' box to record the timestamp for each executed order.

Optionally, create a centralized output directory for transcripts.

This directory should be a registered, restricted network share accessible by security staff. If there is no output directory, transcript files are generated under the user's directory records.

Alternatively, setting the following log values enables:»
HKLM\SOFTWARE\Wow6432Node\Policies\Microsoft\
Windows\PowerShelle\Transcription:»
HKLM\SOFTWARE\Wow6432Node\Policies\Microsoft\
Windows\PowerShell\Transcription
\PowerShell\Transcription= EnableInvocationHeader= 1»

Log Settings

Where appropriate, Mandiant suggests that all three log sources be allowed: logging module, logging block script, and transcription. Each of these sources records unique data that are useful for PowerShell research. Without significantly increasing log size, allowing block logging and transcription of the script records most of its operation, thus minimizing the amount of log data generated. To detect attacker commands and code execution, script block logging should, at a minimum, be allowed.

Ideally, you can add a 1 GB (or as big as your company allows) of the PowerShell event log Microsoft-Windows-PowerShell percentage to make sure data is preserved for a reasonable period. PowerShell logging generates large volumes of data that rolls the log quickly (up to 1 Mb per minute during typical admin or attacker operation was observed).

The Windows Remote Management (WinRM), Microsoft-Windows-WinRM 4Operational.evtx log tracks WinRM connections inbound and outbound, including PowerShell remote links. The log records the source (inbound connections) or destination (outbound connections) and the authentication username. This link data can be useful for lateral tracking with PowerShell remote control. Ideally, the WinRM log should be set to at least one year of data to be stored.

Because of the large number of events generated by PowerShell logging, organizations should consider carefully which events they want to forward to a log aggregator. For PowerShell 5.0 environments, organizations will find, as a minimum, the aggregation, and monitoring of suspicious script block logging incidents, EID 4104 in a SIEM or other log monitoring device with level "alert." Such incidents provide the best opportunity to recognize conflict facts while maintaining a small dataset.

POWERSHELL VS COMMAND PROMPT

PowerShell vs. Command prompt is like comparing kumquats with apples. They are completely different, although the' dir' command functions the same way in both interfaces. They are entirely different.

PowerShell uses cmdlets that are autonomous software objects that display the underlying management options inside Windows. To find these options, sysadmins used the GUI before PowerShell, and there was no way to replicate the interface to change options on a large scale by clicking on the menus.

PowerShell uses pipes to chain cmdlets and shares input/output data, just like other shells like Linux bash. Pipes allow users to create complex scripts that transfer data and parameters from cmdlet to cmdlet. Users can create reusable scripts to automate or change the mass of variable data–for example, a list of servers.

The ability to create aliases for different cmdlets is one of the (many) cool features of PowerShell. Aliases allow a user to set his names for various cmdlets or scripts, making it easier for a user to move between different shells:' ls' is a Linux bash command which displays directory objects, like the' Dir' command. The' ls' and' dir' in PowerShell are an alias of the cmdlet' Get-ChildItem.' The command-line Windows Command Prompt is a basic Win32 application. It can interact in Windows with any other Win32 program or object. People use it for different reasons–but primarily by using software such as System File Checker to adjust vital Windows settings and to patch various operating system components. It can also be named loosely as the revamped MS-DOS version. Before the Command Prompt program was released, MS-DOS was Microsoft's Command Line on Windows Operating Systems application.

The Windows PowerShell command-line interacts more tightly and facilitates scripting with the Windows Operating System. It was released in 2006 and is based on the.NET Platform. This is used for all the functions that the Prompt command can do–but it is also a great tool for system administrators.

The initial difference is that Power Shell uses the so-called cmdlets. Such cmdlets allow the user to perform administrative tasks such as managing the registry to use the Windows Management Instrument. The Command Prompt can not perform such functions. You will learn about Variables if you have even a little exposure to computer programming. These variables are used to store data that can be used for various operations. The PowerShell cmdlets can be used for other cmdlet operations. This allows the merger of several cmdlets to create a complex but powerful cmdlet which performs a task once and for all. As mentioned previously, cmd is an ancient tool that has never been developed for remote system administration. Additional utilities like Microsoft Sysinternals PsExec are necessary to expand its functionality.

On the other hand, PowerShell offers a large range of cmdlets for simplifying system management tasks. It supports the automation of various tasks, such as administration of Active Directory, management of users and permissions, and the extraction of security configuration data. Also, PowerShell supports Linux now.

The table below summarizes the key differences between Command Prompt and PowerShell from a programming and operational point of view: Windows PowerShell provides a great scripting environment for the development and administration of various PowerShell scripts using the extension.ps1 with Windows PowerShell ISE.

The Windows Prompt command can not do all this. It is a legacy environment that is being transferred to modern versions of Windows. It is based on MS-DOS but has little access, as Windows PowerShell does, to administrative privileges.

What is the Command Prompt on Windows PC?

Prompt is known as CMD for Windows Orders. It is a command shell based on the operating system MS-DOS. This GUI allows users to interact directly with the operating system. This means that users can change the operating system and its features using different commands.

It creates a new framework for users and developers to test various applications and other utilities effectively. Interestingly, you will instantly receive the response from the operating system in the same window. You can use the CMD Shell to create additional scripts and save them as batch files if you are on the developing side. You can use the CMD shell. These batch files can be used in a single frame to address automation tasks. It operates manually, and the command lines must be inserted manually in the program. You will have to focus on the commands that are consistent with that particular task on a Windows system if you want to do things automatically.

The Prompt Window command demonstration is given below. You can see how the command lines and answers are described in a single window for each command. It is a simple black window with white fonts. To enter the order, you can use normal keyboards and press the Enter button to receive the answer instantly.

The Prompt command is based on MS-DOS but has nothing to do with the MS-Dos Operating System. It is an autonomous platform that does not rely on other operating systems.

What is the Windows PowerShell on a Windows PC?

Windows PowerShell is also a scripting language-driven command base. This command shell is designed for system administration tasks that allow you to change or build scripts for Windows 10.

The Windows PowerShell is designed using the. NET Framework, so it is more powerful than the prompt Framework for commands. A.NET Architecture is a software development platform that Microsoft itself developed in 2002. Developers use the same apps and other Windows-powered applications design platform.

Cmdlets are also known as PowerShell Commands. You may easily use this Command Shell window if you want to modify or communicate with the Windows Operating System infrastructure.

PowerShell enables users to access the Windows registry as opposed to the Command Prompt Interface. Users can also communicate with the Windows Management System and the file system. Interestingly, all these command lines and features can be used by users remotely. Because the command interface is powerful, users can create complex scripts that can be used for different automation tasks. You can also construct multi-condition scripts.

The Windows PowerShell example can be seen in the image below. The PowerShell has a dark blue window that is entirely different from the Command Prompt window, in contrast to the simple black window.

How Command Prompt Differs from Windows PowerShell

Command Prompt is based on an old MS-DOS system, which becomes an outdated tool for Windows users of the new generation. This control system has been designed for manual tasks and has never been designed for remote management. Users need to add more compatible tools and scripts manually to improve their functionality and functionalities.

On the other hand, PowerShell relies on the advanced .NET Platform of Microsoft, which offers the advanced command-line interface for users and developers who can check the latest software and applications requiring the command-line and its environment.

This Command-Line Gui is designed to simplify administrators ' tasks. It is designed for remote management. A wide range of automation activities is assisted by the same GUI, which can solve both applications and software problems.

The Windows PowerShell is compatible with a range of tasks, deals with active directory management, collect security data and settings, and also manages user permissions. The latest updates also added additional Linux Operating System support.

Contrary to the standard PowerShell window, Windows 10 comes with a PowerShell ISE incorporated, i.e., an Integrated environment for scripting. Its framework is designed for professional developers who can create complex and modern scripts for all apps and applications. Two separate Windows are equipped with the Unified Scripting Framework from which the right-hand window shows essential scripting scripts from the set. Scripts and commands are ready for use, and when working on a new script or checking a command line, you will start using these scripts and commands.

Windows PowerShell is undoubtedly more powerful than the current Prompt order, but it costs you a little. Unlike the simplest commands for the Command Prompt interface, you need to understand the basic functionality for PowerShell and its cmdlets. It's a bit challenging, and you have to spend time learning the new interface.

Which One Is Better?

With WindowsYou would see the Microsoft command prompt interface replaced as the default command-line interface with the Windows PowerShell interface. The old command-line GUI in the new Windows operating system has many reasons to be replaced.

The Windows PowerShell is the new Command Line interface and is compliant with all Command Prompt commands. You can use the command Prompt on the PowerShell window and function with it. If you work on Power Shell, you don't need to switch between GUI. The only thing to do to replace Command Prompt with PowerShell is to simplify the process for developers who can work remotely for an administration function. Unlike the Command Prompt, system administrators can work remotely and complete their tasks quickly.

PowerShell provides a better-known experience than the Prompt Command. In reality, it is much easier to handle various tasks that are necessary for the new generation of applications and apps, despite their flexibility and skill.

Also, all the new generation developers use Windows PowerShell and therefore has a very helpful community that can help you learn new things, or you can even start with basic things by engaging with community members if you're a beginner. You have to continue using the latest and sophisticated command-line interface to keep yourself up to date with new technology and the environment. PowerShell Windows.

Microsoft Is Replacing The CMD Prompt With Powershell

The Command Prompt, one of the last remnants of the ancient MS-DOS days, looks like an endangered species. Windows PowerShell, first implemented on a Windows Server, front and core, was installed in the new Windows 10 preview.

Construct 14791, which the Redstone 2 update is expected to take place early next year, replaces the Command Prompt window in many key areas of the operating system. There is still Command Prompt, not as available. Microsoft uses PowerShell as its primary forward shell command. PowerShell replaces command Prompt ("cmd.exe") in WIN + X, the File Explorer menu, and in the context menu when you press the File Explorer whitespace. The quick way to open the command shell at this position is still to type "cmd" or "PowerShell" in the address bar of File Explorer.

Overall, the Build 14791's updates are quite modest: Edge EPUB books, the Pain 3D edition demo, Chinese and Japanese character enhancements, and a Get Office software update. Redstone 2 is expected to ship next April. This follows a pattern that we saw in Windows 10, where old features are reduced but not eliminated. Internet Explorer 11 exists, but you must manually operate it. The new Edge browser begins with the IE icon in the Task Bar.

Likewise, the control panel is updated by Microsoft. Some build, what you have modified when you use the Power Menu. Instead of the Control Panel shortcut, the full options menu now matches the applet set of the Control Panel.

APPLICATIONS OF POWERSHELL

Often, for some reason, you may have to update your operating system freshly. In this scenario, all applications on the computers are deleted. If you have large numbers of applications on your computer, you probably want the list of applications on your computer mounted. The list lets you record all of your computer's essential apps, and you can install them whenever you want. However, a PowerShell script will make your work easier. This script lists the apps on your computer and saves them on the C drive. You will shift the list to another position from the C drive. It can be your USB flash disk, cloud, another drive, etc. Windows reinstallation is a perfect way to solve your computer's serious problems or to get a new slate. Nevertheless, you can list the programs you have already installed on your computer before reinstalling Windows to decide what you want to reinstall on the new system.

It is also useful to have a list of installed programs if you just bought the new computer and want to run the same programs on your old computer.

HOW TO USE POWERSHELL TO LOCATE A SPECIFIC APPLICATION

Alphabetize the Application List

One way to simplify the application location method is to alphabetize the list of applications. PowerShell provides native sorting features and can be used to build an application list. This is how it works:

Get-Wmi-Object -Class Win32_Product | Sort-Object -Property Name | Select-Object Name

Sort the List by Vendor

Another way to narrow a list of applications is to find apps from a similar manufacturer.

You can do this in several different ways. One possible option is to list the vendor name next to the client name and alphabetize the list by the name of the vendor. This is the command to perform the task: Get-WmiObject -Class Win32 Product Sort-Object -Property Vendor Select-Object Vendor, name As an alternative, you will select a specific vendor by name. Let's assume for a moment I had to figure out what VMware program was installed on my computer, for whatever reason. I would be able to use the following command to do so: Get-WmiObject-Class Win32 Product Where-Object{$. Vendor -Match "VMware"} Select-Object Vendor, Name before going on, I want to point to the above figure. Looking at the top part of the table, you can see the bottom half of the list of applications sorted by the vendor I created before. When you look at that list, the command that I used when I returned the list of VMware software that was installed on my machine searches for the word "VMware," not "VMware, Inc.," but the reason I got rid of it was because I used the -Match operator inside the command rather than using the-EQ operator. The-EQ operator needs an exact match, while the -Match parameter requires that the specified text appear somewhere inside the property you are searching for. If the command had used-EQ instead of-Match, no results would have been returned, because "VMware" does not exactly match the names of any of the vendors on the list. I would have to say "VMware, Inc." as the name of the seller if I chose to use-EQ.

One More Trick

Let me wrap up stuff by showing you another trick that could benefit those without such a great memory.

Let's say I want to uninstall an application for a moment, but I can't remember the name of the program or who makes the application. What I recall was a "V" in the name of the seller. Perhaps the seller was VMware. Maybe it was AVG. I can't remember that. I can't remember that. One way you can deal with this kind of situation is by using the same strategy as I showed you, but use the letter "V" and an asterisk. Any vendor with a V in its name can be found. Here's the order: Get-WmiObject-class Win32 Product Where-Object{$. Vendor-Match "VM*"} Select-Object Vendor, Name You can remember that I'm searching for VM* instead of V* when you see this instruction. This is because PowerShell seems to have a bug. If you use V*, the letter V tends to be ignored. When using VM*, PowerShell forget the letter M and send you the performance you expect to see if you've used V*.

The List Of Installed Programs

Saving the list of programs configured is an important component of the backup strategy. Suppose you have a Windows malfunction or any device problem all of a sudden and have to reinstall Windows. You will miss all the programs built on your device after reinstalling the OS.

If you have a list of the applications that you have installed, you can quickly reinstall it by remembering which programs you had before.

Through PowerShell Command

Users can easily get a list of all installed programs by entering a simple PowerShell command. Please enter PowerShell into the start menu and open the first test. You'll be on your PowerShell Screen to display all installed programs with the date and name of the publisher. The next move is to export this list to another venue. Again paste the same command and after this command write;

Get-ItemProperty HKLM:\Software\Wow6432Node\Microsoft\Windows\CurrentVersion\Uninstall* Select-Object DisplayName, DisplayVersion, Publisher, InstallDate-Table –AutoSize > C:\Users\MahamMukhtar\Documents\InstalledPrograms-PS.txt

And the file will be saved into required folder. File format will be text file.

Through command line

Open as Administrator your Command-Line. And enter the order below.

Wmic users will receive name, version and you will soon see all the installed programs and their version promptly in the command line. And then, after "wmic: root\cli," add the following command/output: C:/InstallList.txt, get name, version.

Then the list will be saved to your system's C drive.

Through ccleaner

CCleaner is a simple tool to improve the efficiency of your Computer by deleting such unwanted and temporary files. The CCleaner tool can also list all of your system's installed programs.

When the update has been opened, go to tools and press Uninstall, and the list of all programs that are installed on your device will appear. To "save as txt file" click.

You will then be asked to save this txt file wherever you want in your program.

Through control panel

All your installed programs can also be accessed easily via' Control Panel," Programs' and' Uninstall a program.' Now you can take a screenshot of it and save it anywhere in your setup, so you will be able to see your installed software later on if appropriate.

All of them are useful and straightforward ways to view and save all installed programs in text format or snapshot format anywhere on your device.

View Windows Updates Size In Windows 10

Windows 10 allows you to download updates, even in the background quickly. The installation of these updates won't bother your job or scare you. But sometimes, you use a limited Internet data plan, and the updates are very large, so you need to keep an eye on the scale of updates. Windows do not provide the default update scale. To define the scale of changes, you must use a third-party tool. I allow you to view the Windows Update Size in your Windows 10.

Windows Update minitool

Windows Update MiniTool is a small portable 32-bit and 64-bit tool available. The best thing about this is that it shows you not only the size of the previous update but also the size of the update you have. You can, therefore, determine whether or not to download the update depending on the size of the update and your data set.

When you install it, a window opens that displays installed updates or updates available, selects one of them, expands the window, and shows you all of the related information, including updates.

It has many apps for you to perform. Those apps include:

Checks for updates that are not available.

Install updates that are not installed.

Download and install updates

Show updates Uninstall updates.

It is an easy and simple application that can support you a great deal and save your data by providing you with the size and the motivation for each update. Overall, Windows Update MiniTool is a smart tool that will help if you don't want to take too much bandwidth from your Windows updates. Either you can altogether disable Windows Update, or you can limit the updates available for download.

WAYS TO VIEW AND SAVE LIST OF UPDATES INSTALLED ON WINDOWS 10

Usually, no administration is needed for Windows Update. Microsoft makes it very much like a compilation and forgets about it. Nevertheless, specific applications require some hotfixes and upgrades on your device before they are running. For instance, some applications require a particular version. NET Framework, redistributable Visual C++ or JAVA, etc. And some applications require hotfixes rather than add-ons.

Using windows update history

Go to Settings for Windows (Windows Key + I

Go to Update & Protection

Select Windows Update from the left menu and click on History Update Link from the right

All updates installed on your Windows 10 machine are shown. The changes will be marked as follows:

Quality updates

Driver updates

Definition updates

Other updates

The only warning when using this tool is that a particular version can not be searched. You must go through the update list manually.

Using Command-line options – DISM/systeminfo

Two commands can be used to extract information from the system from Windows updates. Let's refer to them one at a time.

DISM Run the following command to get all the hotfix details on your device.

You can format output as a table too so that it is easy to read and understand. Wmic qfe list complete

When complete information is not needed, you can use the command following to obtain a summary: wmic qfe list brief. And if you wish to find a particular hotfix, execute the command: wmic qfe list brief "KB4495667" To save the entire output to a file, run the following command: wmic qfé full list/format: table > C:\Users\Usman\Desktop\WindowsUpdatesReport.ht

Open Command Prompt

Run the following command

systeminfo | find "KB"

Using PowerShell

It is easier to obtain the same details from the command line in PowerShell.

Create a PowerShell with administrative privileges

Operate the following command:

Get-Hotfix

This lists all hotfixes on the machine and displays every hotfix's installation date.

Using Winupdateslist

WinUpdatesList is a program from a third party that can be used for the same purpose. It can be used from a network location because it is a lightweight device. The main advantage of using WinUpdatesList is that it lists all available improvements from Windows Updates, hotfixes, changes to Windows Defender definition,.NET System updates, driver updates, etc. The update can also be saved as a CSV format. You will be notified of each update, such as name, installation date, installed by (if you are on the domain network), update sort, link to online hotfix page, uninstall order, last updated, etc.

FILES

A file is a named block of information (byte sequence) stored on a storage medium. A file is the smallest unit of information stored on a medium. The file has the following features:

fixed name (filename) - a sequence of characters that uniquely characterizes a file;

a specific logical image (determined by the type of information contained in the file) and the corresponding read / write operations;

file size (characterized by the size of the information contained therein).

Working with files can be divided into three main steps:

Opening a file;

Work with file-related information (read / write);

Close the file.

When working with files, binary (or binary) and text files are distinguished. Binaries are opened as a byte sequence. The responsibility for correct data handling rests entirely with the program using the file. Text files are opened as a sequence of strings (characters) contained in the file. In this case, the physical string in the file corresponds to the string literal in the program. Generally, you can only create, modify, and edit binaries using a custom program. You can work with text files with any text editor.

OPENING THE FILE

The file is opened by the instruction

f = open(file_name, mode)

where f is the name of the file variable, file_name is the name of the file being opened, mode
- file mode is a string literal that is constructed using the values in the table.

DESCRIPTION AND MODE ON FILE

"r": Opening for reading. If a file with this name does not exist, the instruction generates an error (default value).

"w": Opens to write. If a file with this name already exists, the file will be overwritten with a new one.

"x": Opening for recording. If a file with this name already exists, the instruction generates an error.

"a": Opens to add data to the end of the file.

"+": Opening to read and write.

"b": Binary Opening

"t": Opens in text mode (default).

The mode value is obtained by combining the values above. For example, "rb" is to open an existing binary file for reading. "r" and "t" are the default values and can be omitted when forming mode mode. The default value of the mode parameter is "rt".

The open instruction identifies the contents of file file_name with the variable f. Further file handling is only due to this variable. In addition, the open statement blocks the file for changes by other programs to avoid conflicts.

CLOSING THE FILE

As mentioned above, a file is handled through a file variable that stores its data in RAM. You must close the file to save the result of working with the file on the storage medium. In addition, the file closure operation tells the operating system that the file is unlocked and can be used (to be modified) by other programs. The instruction is used to close the file

f.close(

where f is the name of the file variable associated with the file.

FILE OPERATIONS

Opening a file creates a special object (owned by a file variable) called a marker. The token indicates the current position in the file, which is the place from which the data is read or written.

When opening a file in "a" mode (adding), the marker is set to the position after the last recording. For other modes, the marker is set to the very first record. Any read / write operation changes the current marker position.

Let f be a file variable associated with the file open in the appropriate mode. Then

File operations

f.read () :Returns the entire contents of the file.

f.read (n): Reads n bytes from the current marker position.

f.readline (): Reads and returns the current line from a text file.

f.readlines (): Returns a list of all lines of a text file.

f.write (s): Writes the value of variable s into a file.

print (s, file = f): Writes the value of the variable s into a file.

f.writelines (lineslist): Writes a list of lineslist lines to a text file.

f.tell (): Returns the value of the current marker position in the file.

f.seek (n): Sets the marker to n in the file.

TEXT FILES

A file variable for a text file is a collection of its lines. Therefore, you can pass the text file in rows using the for loop.

```
for line in f:
 process_iteration
```

Let f be a file variable open for reading a text file. Then the instruction

performs process_iteration for all lines of file f.

Here are some examples that illustrate how text files work.

CONCLUSION

In this book, you've learned the basics about operating with PowerShell, the Windows command-line interface. You know enough about using PowerShell for many of the daily tasks you do on your computer, and I would recommend that you use it for that. At first, you may find it harder to copy a file and move it from the command line to a new directory, but the more you practice, the more intuitive it becomes. Finally, you can work in PowerShell very comfortably and can do other things more quickly.

Although we just saw what PowerShell could do, you now have the basic knowledge to learn to do more. It is helpful to know also that a lot of debate will be focused on Unix and other* nix systems about using the command line. If you only type the names of the commands they use in the search engine with "PowerShell," you can find the corresponding PowerShell cmdlet.

The more PowerShell you use, the faster it is, and the more power you gain to open your computer, you don't even know! You will finally see how restrictive your Interface was. You will not stop using it, but you will gradually find yourself starting up PowerShell to break free of those restrictions and use your computer more completely. Your machine is like a knife of a pocket. Just a few blades can be opened in the GUI. You can open them all with the command line!

Do Not Go Yet; One Last Thing To Do

If you enjoyed this book or found it useful, I'd be very grateful if you'd post a short review on Amazon. Your support really does make a difference, and I read all the reviews personally so I can get your feedback and make this book even better.

Thanks again for your support!